In the Days of Our Endurance

NATHAN BROWN

MEZCALITA
PRESS

FIRST EDITION, 2023 (3rd printing)
Copyright © 2023 by Nathan Brown
All Rights Reserved
ISBN-13: 978-1-7348692-8-6

Library of Congress
Control Number: 2023935686

No part of this book may be performed, recorded, thieved, or otherwise transmitted without the written consent of the author and the permission of the publisher. However, portions of poems may be cited for book reviews—favorable or otherwise—without obtaining consent.

Cover Design: Jen Rickard Blair

Mezcalita Press, LLC
Norman, Oklahoma

In the Days of Our Endurance

NATHAN BROWN

Table of Contents

How They Are Made ... 3
Old Souls and Dogs ... 4
How Could They Not ... 6
What We Bring ... 8
I Should Have Listened ... 10
Two Kinds ... 11
His Daily Grind ... 12
Can You Feel It? ... 14
What's That About? ... 16
O Country! My Country! ... 17
A Month Shy of 80 Years ... 20
Though We Try ... 22
Harbinger ... 23
And She Was Ours ... 24
9/11 ... 26
What Might Save Us ... 27
For the Love'uh ... 30
Whiskey and Weed ... 32
I Want More ... 34
Tending Joy ... 36
More Like Sand ... 38
Decomposition ... 40
A Throne of Thorns ... 42
Shoes to Fill ... 43
Look No Further ... 44
If a White Horse ... 46
No Matter What... ... 48
Strategy ... 50

Cocoon ... 51
Agelast ... 52
Know This ... 53
Y'ain't from Around Here ... 54
Mesquite ... 56
Better Watch Out ... 58
Revenants ... 60
Epiphany ... 61
And on the Last Day ... 62
Smelling It Out ... 64
A Saint for Everything ... 66
Or, Orange ... 68
Twice, at Least ... 70
The Richer Fields ... 71
The Nature of Work ... 72
Any *Who* in There? ... 74
Like a Snowflake ... 76
Sinking In ... 77
Stone and Fire, Sun and Moon ... 78
Snap Snap ... 80
Freedom Bath ... 82
Is It Worth Losing Sleep Over? ... 84
Not Fair ... 86
What I Can ... 88
The Least of These ... 90
The Reluctant Invader ... 91
For Your Consideration ... 92
Our Representatives ... 94
This, at Least ... 96
In Threes ... 97
It's Tricky ... 98

One Thing Leads to an Otherwise ... 100
A Working Title ... 102
Just There ... 104
A Simple Abundance ... 106
The Lucky Among Us ... 108
Brother, Father, Friend ... 109
Who Else ... 110
A Good Choice ... 112
The Job ... 114
Here, Where... ... 116
Imitating Art ... 119
This Dance ... 120
Allways ... 121
An Elevated Soul ... 122
We Never Know ... 124
If It Weren't Too Late ... 126
The History of a Hug ... 128
What Time We Have ... 130
Because It Has to Be Said ... 131
#4305 ... 132
Bringing It Back ... 134
Finding Peace ... 135
I Know It Seems ... 136
Psalm 151 ... 138
Psalm 152 ... 140
Son of a Bundy ... 142
Modus Operandi ... 144
For Grace and Baby Courage ... 146
Crucial ... 148
Nicely Done ... 150
Of the American Dream ... 151

Denouement ... 152
Good Mister Secretary ... 154
The Night ... 158
Legacy ... 160
And to My Daughter ... 162
Not Just Any Hat ... 164
A Case of You ... 165
Fire in the Blood ... 166
Corinthians Chapter 13
    for the Darker Soul ... 168
As You Say Grace ... 170
To You Who Does Not Like That I Write
    in the First Person Point of View ... 172
What Gives Us Away ... 174
Burn While Ye May ... 176
Becoming John Denver ... 178
A Blessing for a Blessing ... 179
Anchor ... 180
The Unspeakable ... 181
What It Is, and Isn't ... 182
And What if It Is? ... 184
Fermented Honey ... 186
Well-Spring ... 187
Such a Thing ... 188
Spindrifting ... 189
Why Poetry? ... 190
Poetry: An Index ... 192
The Last Poem ... 198
Seriously, the Last Poem ... 200

Acknowledgements

This book is, very simply, dedicated to everyone who has been a part of this project over the last few years—whether by commissioning, donating, listening, or watching the Fire Pit Sessions.

You've kept the ember glowing down in the soul of the artist and performer in me. And I mean, quite seriously, I do not know what I would have done without you.

Few things have affected more how I perceive myself as a poet and writer, as well as what the artist's purpose is in the scope of history. I've been humbled and inspired at the same time. And I have discovered that audience is more than *appreciation*… it is *participation* in art.

~ Nathan

*   *   *

"Though We Try" first appeared in *Boundless 2022*: the anthology of the Rio Grande Valley International Poetry Festival

In the Days of Our Endurance

MEZCALITA
PRESS

How They Are Made

> ~ to a young woman in Afghanistan

There is a smallness in some men
that only a catastrophic interpretation
of God can help them compensate for.

It takes a depraved theology to justify
the amount of nothing in their souls…
the sheer meaningless weight they carry.

And so what can we expect from those
whose main goal in their quixotic lives
is to die a beautiful, vainglorious death?

A thing they crave out of desperate fear
and their unrelenting suspicion that they
are ultimately, and vastly, inferior to you.

Old Souls and Dogs

~ for Lou Kohlman

How late is too late
for old souls to change.
Especially souls not known
to be fans of it.
                But, especially
one well known to not care for it.

Like Tevye, in *Fiddler on the Roof*,
bellowing "Tradition… tradition!"
and shouting at his daughter "No!"
when she wants to marry the gentile.

Some things just should not be done.

Like my parents selling their home
of 50 years and moving to Texas
to live in a 4th-story apartment
at a senior living community
careful not to refer to itself
as a rest home (or worse)…
so they can be closer to kids.

Or, like you… after almost 30
years working in criminal law,
having five days to decide…

whether to follow your judge
from the Court of Appeals to
the Oklahoma Supreme Court.

Five days, and it's pack it up,
move it to a new office, and
start over, doing your best
to avoid out-loud talk about
old dogs and something to do
with… what is it… new tricks?

How Could They Not

> ~ for Guillaume and Erin,
> from Konrad and Darra

We are gathered here
for the wonder and surprise
of what happens when Bumble
actually works. Which isn't always.

But how could she have swiped left
when his profile picture showed him
holding that huge beloved tuba of his.

And since she had played one like it
in her high school marching band,
she knew they'd have one thing,
at least, to talk about on the weird
first date that ensues in these times.

And with him tired of the scene,
how could he not be taken…
if not aback… by her showing
up at the patio of the restaurant
in gym clothes fresh from training
for a half marathon.
                      Which is a more
impressive way to say sweaty and gross.
And which would also be an appropriate

time, it seems, to question the behavior
and motivation of a neuropsychologist.

But to his credit, as a choreographer,
he knew where to place his feet…
as well as when to step back…

because, for him, even though
she offered a good Midwestern
apology for her first impression,
she emitted a certain light and
sizzling energy that could
not be denied.
              And for her,
with her education and training,
how could she not notice the way
he spoke of his students, the regard
he showed, that tiny bit of tearfulness.

But especially the way, on their second
date, he hugged her, something about
the whispered language of his arms.

A man who learns that dialect
will always have a chance.

What We Bring

~ for Guillaume and Erin, on your wedding

We're an odd combination,
that impossible sum, of
protons and electrons,
the pluses, minuses, pros

and cons of those who came
before and around us… those
we came from… and those who
stuck by us—despite the minuses.

And marriage is the great weighing,
where we put the mess on the scales
and decide who we must be in love,
how we should be in life together,
and how we will, and how we
will not, treat each other.

Finding the beautiful balance,
that elemental mote of an atom
that will make the scales float…

is as much art as it is science,
just as much music as math.

And so we're all here today,

dressed in hope, and our most
uncomfortable clothes, to bring
the best we have to offer, to lay
that best down on the scales,

and weigh in.

I Should Have Listened

~ an apology for mom

You tried to warn me,
some seven or more years
ago, you gave me a small tube
of Purell Advanced Hand Sanitizer
that Kills the Most Germs—such
a Refreshing Gel. You told me
sickness and death lurked
in all public restrooms,
on gas pump handles,
but especially within
gas station bathrooms.

And I just now found it
in the drawer in my own
guest bathroom, still full,
and hiding beneath some
hotel soaps, an old comb,
and a pitiful pile of irony.

And, like so much of
your good advice…
it's too late to save me.
It expired in 04 of 2016.

Two Kinds

~ for Danna Primm

I like the thinkers
more than knowers.

Because… the thinkers
are still thinking about it,
while the knowers are done.

For, what is left to think about,
the knowers ask? when we know?

That's why thinkers, while oftentimes
frustrating, are at least more interesting.

Because when the knowers know a thing,
and therefore refuse to think much more
about it, there's nothing left for anyone
to do but finish off that glass of wine
and stare at the dying fire in silence,
while trying not to think about it.

His Daily Grind

~ for Sam and Cathey Lanham

A popular mythology has him
in his floor-length black robe.

I have always imagined a dude
in a zoot suit... white wingtips.

And whether his tool of choice
is the scythe, or a tommy gun...
it's just for melodrama... a prop.

His most productive instruments,
we reinvent for him every century.
Wars, governments, or oxycodone,
autobahns, and interstate highways,

saving pandemics for when he wants
a vacation on his island in that river,
allowing tiny viral bugs do his dirty
work for him while he drinks his
Kamikazes or Molotov cocktails
in a deck chair by the black pool.

But he is back at work now. And
he's hit your neighborhood three
times in a week. He worked over

your beloved Elmer—a 95-year-old
church member—and, he took his
damned time in doing it.
                        And then,
Seattle—a harmless and homeless
schizophrenic who wandered up
and down the streets in Lubbock,
gunned down by gangbangers who
saw him as a form of entertainment.

And, to complete the trinity, a friend
and a favorite massage therapist, "with
healing in her hands," you said, woke up
one morning feeling a bit off, and before
her wife could return from the kitchen
with a cup of coffee… she was gone.
Rest in peace, Erin. You are missed.

We pray, we plead.
                      And he yawns.

What a terrible job it must be.
And, how badly he must
wish to die himself.

Can You Feel It?

~ for Larry Martin

So my friend told his wife,
I am told, to pause Take 130
of the Fire Pit Sessions while he
went inside to patch his margarita…
because he didn't want to miss the part
where I cried. That's happening a lot
these days.
          I'm moving boxes
full of journals, poetry, CDs,
and the unopened shipments
of my own books and albums
that I haven't been able to sell,
along with my wife, the new dog,
and our two middle-aged cats, who
will be none too happy about change,
across and up the road some ten miles.

At the same time, I'll be moving parents
down across the Red River to Texas from
the house they've loved and lived in for 50
years now… the house that oversaw all 17
or so of my broken hearts… the house
I learned to play guitar in, because
of the sixteen girls I loved…

the house where I'd stashed
just as many boxes of memories
and CDs that I couldn't sell either,
because they were an embarrassment.

So, I appreciate that my friend wanted
his wife to pause the show—in order
for him to pour another ounce, or
two, of tequila to help him get
through another one of my
tearful little episodes…

I'd do the same for him.

I'll add, though, that I hope
he will seek out some therapy.

You know, for his tragic inability
to experience, or express, emotion.

WHAT'S THAT ABOUT?

~ for Anne Roberts

I mean… we are
professionals, right?
For decades we've been
performing as if we were,
anyway. I mean… you even
sang at your parents' funerals.
But now that audiences've been
declared a very bad idea for a year
and a half, and we've been singing
to photos and small phone screens,
we seem to have lost that fine edge.
And now songs that we've delivered
a hundred or more times into mics
and bright lights, bring us down
to our knees in a fit of tears…
as if we're listening for the first
time to the words and meaning.
Some we'll likely have to retire.
Others we'll need to practice…
not to relearn and nail the song,
but to keep from crying over it.
Since future audiences will
have enough already
on their plates.

O COUNTRY! MY COUNTRY!

~ for Terry Clark

I sing my own songs…
since Whitman taught me how.
I sing with America, its open roads,
and every electric body that wanders
back and forth between our shores.

I moan with those long slow trains
hauling empty shipping containers
through the dim light of predawn,
mourn the monumental effluence
of the carpet manufacturing industry.

I praise the strong back with no privilege
or advantage working for whatever wages,
the bare minimum the employer can offer
while managing to avoid criminal charge.

I might even praise that lone politician
who votes against guaranteed reelection.

And, with Whitman as my model, even
some conspiracy theorist who breathes
the crowned virus into the young lung
of his only child, before he enters
the ICU, to die on a ventilator.

I sing the sound reasoning
of the hermit—who leaves
behind the noise and greed,
the perpetual glowing creed
of screens that never stop.

But... I most certainly sing
the labial loneliness and sorrow
of a sexually frustrated mother of two,

as I lift up my arms with a heartfelt hymn
to the Fahrenheit fears of next generations,
and the legacy of lunacy we're leaving them.

In light of that... I pray for the previously
housed who were recently made homeless
by the hell-wind and rain of Hurricane Ida.

Which makes me want to praise the nature
conservancy trying to buy the remaining
lots in our neighborhood, because of
the wild amounts of water that no
longer exist beneath the ground.

O America, with your magnificent
mountain ranges and clear-cut forests,
glistening glacial lakes and the slow-rolling

streams no one can drink from anymore,
for hydraulic fracturing and strip mining.

O Country! My Country! with your huge
and scintillating cities, so full of modern
art museums and rampant gun violence,
skyscrapers, gastropubs, and systemic
corruption, discrimination, racism.

O land of the free, yet former home
of the slave, conqueror and annihilator
of the indigenous existing with the Earth,
feet married to the fallen leaves and soil…

    I love and lament you,
        laugh at your lame jokes,
            I loathe your arrogance,
                fear for your downfall…

            and yet, will stand for,
          hold out true hope for,
        with all I have left for…
your possible redemption.

A Month Shy of 80 Years

~ for my aunt, Doris Kemp
(October 22, 1941 to September 3, 2021)

To my memory, hers was a laugh
that would echo into the next day...
a laugh that also covered a good deal
of suffering she mostly kept to herself.

A loyal friend, once she'd chosen you.
A solid sense of humor, named one of
her beloved cats, Mouse. Trained a dog,
so she claimed, to come inside to poop.

As one family story goes, whenever
she came up to Norman to visit us,
she'd make sure to write her birthday
on our calendar hanging on the fridge.

A devout member of the church choir
at First Baptist of Cyril, Oklahoma.
A voice that covered for anyone
who couldn't make it on Sunday.

She traveled outside the country
just one time in 80 years... took
their mother to see the oldest son
who worked in oil over in Bangkok.

Came back to Oklahoma and never left her homeland again... that was plenty for her. Until this evening... when she crossed over the other...

that eternal... shore. By the hand of a pandemic, but in the arms of someone much higher... something much better.

Though We Try

~ for Larry Martin (and his photograph)

When a wall is built
for the proprietary
purposes of people
who believe we can
own pieces of land,

Nature begins her act
of reclamation the very
moment it is completed...

careful to move slowly enough
that the fool who built the thing
will not perceive the inevitable.

HARBINGER

~ for Larry Martin (and his photograph)

More than the show is over
on this late night in New Orleans,
now that The Big Easy ain't no more,
now that the Paris of the South appears
to be perpetually slated for redemolition
every ten to twenty years by whatever
letter in the alphabet is next in line
during hurricane season... yes...

the writing's all over the walls
of the French Quarter, but
no one can read it when
the night is as black
as a spilled ink well.

And She Was Ours

> ~ in memory of my cousin,
> Becky Kennedy Gorczyca
> (November 12, 1958 to February 23, 2021)

Every family needs its warrior,
even if it's a daughter, and even
if she is the youngest in the line
of three… one detail she enjoyed
reminding her brother and sister of
any chance she got. Which was often.

The one who fights for the underdog,
but especially if it happens to be a dog.

The one who cheers on her beloved
Dallas Cowboys… even in the bad
years, when they don't deserve it.

But, certainly the one who takes
that stand for her older sister in
what will be among the truest
challenges the family will face.

The warrior is not the easiest
among us—the hard nature
of her difficult job in life…

the courage it requires,
and the toll it all takes.

A good reason to keep
her animals always close…
they are much more forgiving,
possessing the patience of turtles,
another of her big loves, by the way.
A love she'd held for most of her life.

So, why wouldn't she come back as one,
for a brief visit one morning at 11:11 a.m.
A mysterious minute in the angel hour.

Just a chance to see the redbud tree
that'd been planted in her honor
there in Jake's old sandbox
out in the backyard.

9/11

> ~ on the 20th anniversary

Terrorists come in many forms,
the bruised fruits of bad religion,
dark assassins for angry gods, or
pale sons and daughters of lost
causes and worst case scenarios…
who wear camouflage, for the fear
their lack of color might render them
invisible to the much larger population.

Today, we are reminded of the worse
they could, and likely will, do to us,
unless God decides to cure them
of their diabolical theology.

So… to those who paid
on this day 20 years ago,
for that dull ache of their
absence of a better purpose,

we will keep remembering you,
and keep not forgetting them,
remaining diligent to combat
the horrifying emptiness
that creates them.

What Might Save Us

~ for Kin and Kay Pirtle, from the family

The world's dying to know
what might save it… and,
though opinions may vary,
how can we go wrong with
lives spent, and remembered,
in and for the causes of goodness,
kindness, faithfulness, and generosity.

Those who create a sense of home for
others away from and missing theirs.

Like those young airmen of Biloxi,
or college students up in Oklahoma
navigating a newfound independence.
While remaining the solid encouragers
of their own kids, and grandkids—with
all the band concerts and rock climbing,
tennis matches and soccer games, dance
recitals and the art shows that that entails.

We can trust the man who collects books,
loving most the rare ones. But, especially
the man who actually takes his precious
time to read each and every one as well.

The man who would not
be caught without one, often
reading several at the same time.

We can trust the woman who loves
her horses... who knows in her spirit
and bones... why the Appaloosas
love, and live for, the running.

But certainly a couple committed,
not only to each other, but also
to the making and keeping of
a family's annual traditions...

like opening all the presents
on Christmas Eve, because
dad, the biggest kid, could
not wait to tear into them,

the making of the King Cake
when Mardi Gras rolled around,

but definitely Easters... with that
Easter Bread, and its frosting of
grass and little eggs, the hunts
on the farm, supervised from
a golf cart, Sunday afternoons

hanging out under the carport,
then flying a few colorful kites.

Yes... what might save the world,

is more doctors with the time to talk
when we call, who even listen to us,
who treat the janitors at the hospital
with the same respect extended to
nurses, attendants, or colleagues,

and more good souls who write
and send cards to a list of those
she worries might be lonely...
the widows, or older friends.

There are not enough of you.

But, you somehow make up
for the difference, and lack.

And we are forever grateful.

FOR THE LOVE'UH…

> ~ for Konrad Eek, written by Mark Burr,
> and translated by Nathan Brown

The friend who is patient, thoughtful,
and thorough enough to teach you—

because that's how he is with most
every other thing he does… yet,
not with every other person…
we have noticed—

                      the intricacies
of tying and attaching the fly line
to the backing, then the leader to
the line, the tippet (a hangman's
rope, in late Middle English) to
the leader, the fly onto the tippet,
have mercy, just so the two of you
can go fly fishing in Crested Butte.

But then also how to secure the tiny
fly to the tippet before applying some
stuff called 'floatant,' whatever the hell
that is, to it in order to keep that sucker
riding high on the water—then put it all
with the reel on the rod, and finally how
to work the rod to lift the line up off of

the water with the fly, and then bring
the line overhead, using the rod and
timing to push the line and fly out
over and then onto the water…

again… just for the sole sake
of trout in the Gunnison…

well… that is one true,
and helluva, friend.

WHISKEY AND WEED

~ for Konrad Eek, from Mark Burr

So… the two of you date two girls
who are best friends in high school,
then lose them to time… or maybe
with intent… who remembers how.

But, your friendship is sealed for life.
I mean, two grown-ass men who play
bridge, for godsake. And in Oklahoma,
no less. So you know people were talkin'.

Which led to the river trips—Eleven Point
in Missouri, where you'd let ol' Dan float
for a while, after falling out of his canoe.
You know, to wait for a safer pullout.

The trip where you really roughed it
out there in the wilderness. You know,
by driving into Kansas City to watch ol'
Dr. J play b-ball, then grab some BBQ.

Then, there was the Buffalo River over
in Arkansas that you were warned about
in a gear shop near the take-off point, by
a man, his son, the brother, and a nephew.

Who, in retrospect, may have all been
the same person... I mean, you both
were high as pole vaulters, and had
just watched the movie *Deliverance*.

It was wind-beaten rides in Kon's
open-air Jeep Wrangler, dust-caked
by Montana's Flathead Lake, and damn
near dying on a crumbling mountain road.

It was browns, brookies, and rainbows...
and the man pan-frying them to perfection.
It was the ghostly and heartbreaking beauty
of Yellowstone charred and ashen after fire.

It was also wild turkeys and sweet new rods
from the Grizzly Hackle up in Missoula...
wind shear and the bear bells... whiskey,
weed, and the enlightenment they bring.

It was more than enough to fill a good
lifetime—which makes the possibility
of still more ahead feel like an excess,
lasciviousness, and a damn good idea.

I Want More

~ for Karen Zundel

The album version
doesn't tell bad jokes.

A CD makes no mistake.

The MP3 audio file is nothing
more than a low-quality variation
on an already inferior theme. So, just
another digital step in a wrong direction.

Headphones, speakers, merely translators
that can never quite find the right words.

Back around the mid 1990s, I skipped
an opportunity to hear John Denver
perform live on what I had no idea
would be his final concert tour.
I still wince thinking about it.
My first groovy influence.

And now, all I have left
are these albums, warped
LPs, a plastic pile of CDs,
and my laptop full of MP3s.

Well that, and my mean friend
Beth Wood, who will torture me
on occasion, by spitefully tapping
her middle finger on her cheek…

right where Sir Denver once
gave her a kiss backstage
when she was little.

Tending Joy

> ~ for Lynde and Rusty Myers

The joy of a pearl is born not only
out of that tight-jawed darkness...

but also the dimming, breathless
depths the diver must descend
through to reach the shell.

If it were an easy fruit
hanging on some weed
that grew among cracks
of sidewalks and streets,
we would surely ignore it.

Diamonds form in the deeper
darknesses—and in the throes
of volcanic heat and pressure.

Flour and water have to meet
in fire to become bread, and
yet again, to turn into toast.

So here we are, 20 months
into the 21st Century's first
worldwide, well-engineered
human catastrophe. And...

as one of last century's finer
prophets, William Stafford,
tried to help us understand,

the darkness around us is deep.

Which means, it might be
time to look inward and
begin to tend the seed
germinating down in
the heart's recesses.

More Like Sand

~ for Carole Moody

We compare it to the ocean,
the depth and breadth of it,
or maybe to a flowing river.

But love is more like sand.
It's all around, enchanting
to walk on, along a dry bed,

or a shore, but hard to hold onto
with a clenched fist. And, if it gets
into your shorts? better watch out.

Still, I like it between my toes, for
some odd reason I can't explain.
It lasts forever—but in trillions

and quadrillions of tiny grains
that continually shift around
in the ebb and flow of eons.

We measure time with it too,
as it sifts slowly through that
strangely-shaped hourglass.

We build damp castles out of it,
that the salty waves already have
designs on before we even begin.

It holds us up, unless it's of that
dangerous variety we sink into…
(what scary movies are made of).

It's most beautiful when the sun
rises or sets on it. But we take it
any time of the day we can get it.

And at the end of our earthly days,
we will dissolve back into its arms…
the deep, warm embrace that formed us.

DECOMPOSITION

~ for Danna Primm

My body is teaching me
slowly, though sometimes
quickly, our bones and joints
are subject to a mandate of stiff
limitations… one of mine being:

> *Thou shalt never commit another*
> *round-off back-handspring again.*

I still stack my stones… but I do it
thoughtfully, and very one at a time.

And the stones, I notice, are getting
smaller with each new undertaking.

When I climb up a ladder to clear
a gutter of brown rotting leaves,
it is a conscious endeavor, one
of intentional foot placement.

And, if I ever attempt to lift
a kitchen table or easy chair
on my own, like I used to,
be prepared to call 911…

whatever the ambulance costs.

I've ridden hard and put myself
away wet for half a century now,
invincibility a dead distant dream.

Yet, as the Greeks remind us, even
the gods fizzle out and break down.

The reason I call it a day a bit earlier,
raise a salted glass to them every night.

A Throne of Thorns

~ for Christa Pandey

I suppose it is the way
absolute comfort totally
makes me uncomfortable…
like The Miami Beach EDITION,
a hotel so white, I wrote about it as,
> *Truly, the only place I've seen any whiter*
> *than this was the inside of a padded cell.*

I have no use for a room so pristine
I am nervous to set my margarita
on that table next to the chair.

It also has to do with the way
perfection never quite delivers.
No matter how expensive a hotel,
the shower will still drip, or the eight
pillows will not add up to the right one,
or you'll still find a dead rat on the balcony.
I love the frayed edges of the lived in…
I need a writing table small enough
that it holds no distractions,
and a chair hard enough
that it reminds me
I can't sit here
all damn day,
so get it done.

SHOES TO FILL

~ for Rick Bradfield

"Something you might click to open"
13-Across… in the upper right corner
of *The Times* Sunday crossword puzzle.
You have to wonder if it was the first
three-square answer that he filled in
on that last puzzle he ever solved.

And over a lifetime as a journalist,
he'd solved his share. Some much
messier, more dark and difficult,
than those *Times* saw fit to print,
a paper he might have respected,
but never felt a need to work for.

He did his good work, where he
felt called to do it. So determined
to leave a wake of better journalists.

A calling he took quite seriously…
one he believed our future survival
might truly and terribly depend upon.

That's why the void left in his passing
is so severely quiet, a soul could
hear a pen click.

Look No Further

> ~ in memory of Rick Bradfield,
> from Cassy Burleson

A good man is getting harder to find—
that's why, when we come across one,
we should hold on tighter than ever.

Too few boys are born into nature
these days… hands on the rocks
of the Rockies, holding on hard
to the earth, lips so close to stone,
skis cutting snow on a blank canvas,
a campfire, not for show, but boiling
water, drying socks, and thawing toes.

All led to being an Eagle Scout at 12
and, chances are, down a long road,
a lifelong unslakable thirst for truth,
and sticking to the facts, even when
facing down a Kleagle of the KKK,
or Gloria Steinem, or a disgruntled
1,500-pound buffalo—once again,
nature serving as the great teacher.

Here's a man with both feet solidly
on the ground… a man with such
a command over words, he never

needed many to put a blustering
politician, or pontificating pundit,
back in his sit-down-shut-up place...
a man who knows the power of writing
and reading (three fat books a weekend)
over talking. So, when he does speak,
you turn to listen with your eyes.

This is the man who, when the fire
breaks out, you want him on the job,
and when the big fertilizer plant blows
heaven and hellward, he's who we need
trying not to puke in a low-flying Cessna,
because he will deliver what happened,
who was lost, who will go on hurting,
and who is most likely lying about
what caused that whole debacle.

So if you're looking for good men,
because you fear for the future
without what they bring to it,
hold this one up as an example,
and say to yourself over and again:

More like this one. Yes, more men
who are more like this good man.

IF A WHITE HORSE

> ~ for the Sorenson family
> at Palo Duro Riding Stables

When the sunlit cliff is so high
on the rim above the canyon...
and our distance from it just so
as well... well... if a white horse

then appears, and poses perfectly
above that heavenward escarpment,
in a thin veil of ancient dust and lore,
we know what dreams are dreamed for.

We see the maiden vision that gave birth
to the unicorn... whose hooves leave
no prints... and skip across water...
whose horn serves as the talisman

for the innocence of young girls,
the purest and only human form
a unicorn allows to come near...
for reasons most eventually learn.

And any of us who do not, never
become fully human... this being
the sad race that attempts to cast
doubt on the unicorn's existence.

Ah... but the rest of us... those
souls who still have dreams left
inside our evanescent lives...

well... we know better, and
all it takes is a ten-dollar bill
for us to keep the secret safe.

No Matter What...

~ for Brenda Sebern

we've got some warm days ahead...
and our children's children will need
much stronger brands of sunscreen;

the Brits will always put a kettle on
and have some witty bit of wisdom
Americans should pay attention to;

the wealthy will continue to move
to and spoil a dwindling number
of pristine, majestic, once quiet
landscapes left on this planet...
and the poor will bear the brunt.

No matter what...

I will continue to tell the Southern
Baptists Jesus never really said that;

the poets and painters, bookworms,
bassoonists and bards, the actors and
their extras, the dancers and directors,
the vintners, brewers, and the distillers
of all good fruits, veggies, and grains...
and hell... even the writers of prose...

must get up in the morning and grind
the beans of the roasters and scramble
the eggs or boil the oats of the farmers,
and, for God's sake, keep going to work;

the corporations will never be the humans
their lawyers claim and argue that they are.

No matter what...

Charlie Brown 'n' Snoopy, Linus 'n' Lucy,
Pig-Pen 'n' Peppermint Patty, will be there
on Halloween, Thanksgiving, 'n' Christmas;

politicians will pretend to act on our behalf,
as televangelists will claim to act on God's;

the fire ants, coral snakes, dung beetles,
and the scorpions will survive it all.

And, no matter what...

we each must determine
what *No Matter What* means
for us. Then live as if the hopes
of our children's children ride on it.

STRATEGY

~ for Darra Maxwell-Eek

When war comes to the field of love,
one we did not ask for, brought on
by a neural glitch, throwing sparks
in the interests of no one involved,
we must begin to consider tactics…
especially the ones that'll accomplish
nothing… even though they will be
the most cinematic to dream about.
So, while we load the torpedo bays,
we should keep in mind the good ol'
black and white advice of Ed Beach
in the 1950s – Run silent, run deep.

Take the long view, and remember
that staying quiet and out of sight,
is one of the oldest weapons ever
wielded by generals and parents.
Heads down, holding onto our
passions and helmets, we know
there will be years lost. But… if
the heart that lies on the other side
of the battles and the borderlines
survives life in the dark clutches,
there may come some day when
we cross the minefield unscathed.

COCOON

> ~ for Pam Gunsten

This season of stillness...
safely inside... so necessary...

so many unseen things occurring
that we should not live without...
rushing at this point, certain death.

And even upon the cracking open,
the slow emerging into rude air...
there comes the dangling from,
that hanging on for dear life,
as wings unfurl, stretching
out into an unknown future.

The drill sergeant of our DNA
making sure we pump and flap,
the calisthenics of our nature.

Ask any albatross, or airline
pilot, or ask any monarch,

there is no shortcut to
learning how to fly.

Agelast

~ for Betty Potts

That there's a word
for someone who never
laughs, must mean someone
at some point in time never did.

I think only briefly of that wealthy
young brat in his yellow sweater vest
who isn't going to get the red leather
interior he wanted, hands on his hips.

You know… the one with no excuses.

I think longer on that teenaged girl
who's got terribly good reasons…
she is a hard-rock case of things
that go wrong in so many men.

You know… the one with all
the excuses we cannot bear.

Then there's Vladi Putin…
who even when he appears
to laugh, his eyes still frown.

As for us, what's our excuse?

KNOW THIS

~ for the know-it-all

Sometimes, I am you.
But this isn't about me.
This is about you, which
is all you've ever wanted.
What's confusing, I know,
is that while you may know
all there is to know, you can
know it all and still be wrong.

What's worse is that later in life
you'll come to know something
that goes against an other thing
you were once just so sure about,
and now you're left with an awful
and disorienting realization that…
you may not have known something,
which for one who knows everything
can shake the earth beneath your feet.
A good time to stop and think before
you begin to know something else…
or else you'll just go on knowing it all
while everyone you know becomes
less and less willing to bear it all.
Take it from me… I know.

Y'AIN'T FROM AROUND HERE

~ Daryl Ross Halencak

In the country that is Texas,
each county counts a state…
and so it is the State of Foard
puts you just north of Truscott,
east of Paducah, west of Lockett,
and down beneath the quandaries of
Quanah, Chillicothe, Medicine Mound.

And if you hail from the north or east,
or anywhere else, really, possessing
a firm, and ridiculous, stereotype
of what you think the Lone Star
nation is about, Foard County
will surely feed your distastes.

Here, where the main attraction
of most towns is the local cemetery.
Here, where cows, cactus, and blowing
dirt outnumber you by the thousands,
millions, and billions, respectively.

And, you'll catch a strong whiff
of all three in the hash browns,
eggs, and black coffee down
at Taters, on 1st Street…

but know that everyone
else who's sittin' in there
can smell what's on you—
yeah, they know the stench
of Y'ain't-from-around-here
as well, or better, than anybody.

And also, keep in mind that for every
redneck asshole you spot who confirms
your prejudices, there are five to seven
decent and solid folks, tough citizens
of a hard land, who would compete
with the stock you come from any day.

Those rare individuals who'd take you
into their homes and feed you protein
if your car broke down, somewhere
on one of their gravel roads. And,
they'd do it despite being aware
of your silly misconceptions.

MESQUITE

~ for Terry Clark

It's that grumpy neighbor
across and down the road
who's never going to take
that shit, the yellowy shells
of rotting campers, tractor
parts, and rusted bumpers,
out of his uncut front yard.

It's that brooding Chicano
in a dark corner of the bar
with a deadly glare—a shiv
up every sleeve, and a head
full of the damn good reasons
that we have supplied him with.

And, like the cockroaches, it—
with those long-ass roots digging
so far down to the ever-shrinking
water table—will well out-survive
our species in its self-destruction.

And, like Jesus, we can crucify it
with a bloody crown, then cut it
down to the ground, and it will
as often as not, just rise again.

Loving a desert since the Pliocene,
it laughs at our computer-generated
needs for swimming pools, hot tubs,
golf courses, and gaudy hotel-casinos
with manmade rivers running through.

And in Chapter 15 of *Walter Benjamin
at the Dairy Queen*, Larry McMurtry
claims his two biggest fears as a kid
were "poultry and shrubbery," more
specifically, beaks and thorns… since
he goes on to say that his "first lesson
was that human beings were peckable."
He rated these two concerns above
snakes and bulls, even stampedes.

And, if it takes hold in a bristly
stand, somewhere in a section
of your land, your odds are as
good as the Texans' in those
last few days of the Alamo,
if you hope to defeat it.

BETTER WATCH OUT

~ for Anne Roberts

We all know at least one...
the Bah-ers and Humbug-ers
who enjoy the Christmas season
for the opportunity it supplies them
to crank the volume on their general
disbelief in things...
                        the ones who
agreed with Bill Murray in *Scrooged*,
right up to that eye-rolling moment
of his totally over-the-top epiphany...

those who make fun each year of Zuzu
when the bell rings on Christmas Eve
in that scene of *It's a Wonderful Life*.

There's an Ebenezer in every past,
you can bet. The great curmudgeon
who transcends gender, philosophy,
and every denominational creed...

and yet... when a good friend
with an angel's voice begins
to sing that age old hymn
"Sweet Little Jesus Boy"
they bow their heads.

And when that friend
reaches the age old lines,

> *But please sir, forgive us Lord.*
> *We didn't know who you were.*

an eyelid starts to twitch and quiver,
and soon, they're fighting the urge
to run throw open some window
and shout to a ragamuffin below
to run buy that big prize turkey
hanging in the poulterer's shop.

Revenants

~ for Brady Peterson

A tiny nib of pencil lead
has been lodged in the fleshy
crook between my right thumb
and forefinger since my early 20s.

I can go without noticing it sometimes
for decades by now. And as I get older,
it's disappearing behind the rough work
of my hands with stones—the calluses
of earthy wounds, which, inexplicably,
make me think of it more often lately.

It's the same with her, and my heart.
Not a feeling, but more of a presence,
and not anything I'm trying to dig out,
or up, from underneath these stones.

It's far too late to worry about it…
and though there is a slow fading,
inside a lifetime of love wounds,

I know she will never be
all the way gone.

Epiphany

~ for Karen Zundel

We could use a few wise men,
star-chasers, with their eyes on
the skies and ears to the ground,

who would remind us that bad
leadership abounds everywhere,
and who would warn us of which

ones are losing their despotic minds,
and so are about to start murdering
every child under the age of two.

When I think of King Herod,
some 2,000 years ago, I cannot
help but think of Vladimir Putin,

here in 2022, which makes me think
of Sir Charles Darwin and the two
or four questions I have for him.

Because… if his theory holds…
it seems we should've had, by now,
more than just those three wise men.

And on the Last Day

~ for Danna Primm

And on the seventh day
God rested from his work.
For it wholly wore him out…

so much so, that he continued
to rest for thousands of years.

Which gave us time to scatter
the celestial light he'd created
by gorging the firmament with
hot gases and heavy particulates,
those beautiful contrails blocking
the obnoxious view of heaven…

which we accomplished by
clear-cutting all the plants
yielding seed and the trees
bearing fruit of every kind,
for to pave it with concrete
and petroleum-based asphalt,
so we could drive our QX80s,
Dodge Rams, and Hummer H1s
all over the dry land he'd gathered
into places to separate the waters…

waters which we could not
leave unblemished either,
so, we poured, drained,
and spewed every type
of nuclear, chemical,
microbiological, and
crude-oil effluence
known to our kind
in its rivers and seas.

And so, here in the last days,
God looks out over everything
he had made… and… well…

Smelling It Out

~ for Amy Robinson, from Anne Harris

A good dog knows a good thing
when it smells it. But especially
a good person... those certain
souls who know the soul of a dog
is truer than those of most humans.

Those exceptional people, the free
spirits... the whisperers... who
understand that long walks
twice a day are not about
exercise, for god sake...
they're about the glorious
traces and intriguing scents
left behind by fellow travelers.

(The good nose God gave a dog
being an organ humans will never
know the power of, in their sad
and totally sight-driven lives.)

These are rare warriors, who fight
for the rights of all good animal souls,
rescue, watch over, and watch out for
the neglected... feeding the hungry,

and housing the poor when winter
sinks its teeth in and shakes them.

And so all a good dog really wants
for Christmas is one of these holy
hearts to love them.
                       Well…
that… and… maybe a brand new
shiny red Santa Clause squeaky toy.

A Saint for Everything

~ for Shayla Dodge

Sometimes…
when Saint Drogo,
the patron of caffeine,
smiles… we find, down
at the bottom of a hot cup
of kindnesses, and very finely
French-pressed coffee, a friend.

And, as a string of recent struggles
slowly unwinds into a kind of easing,
there comes, with every mug he makes
every morning, steeped in fresh-ground
beans from places that matter to him…
seems Brazil was one… this exquisite
precision and taste, all stirred in with
a heaping teaspoon of compassion.

And now, each morning's made
a bit brighter by an unexpected
wit, intelligence, and ceremony
in his retirement, next door,
and on your daily ways to
work that must be done.

So… with his earthbound
angel in place, Saint Drogo
folds his arms, leans back in
to his holy rocker and rolls it,

as he reaches over for his own
thermos of God's finest roast.

Or, Orange

~ for Cathey Lanham

So a friend tells me
that Lubbock, Texas
has a color quandary—
as in a notable lack of it.
How I remember Moscow.

I'll have to look closer next time
I drive the grid of those gray streets.
But she should know; she's lived here
35 years—and Amarillo before that.

So, she's had some time to think
about the special idiosyncrasies
of a panhandle that God built
out of a single piece of caliche.

Calcium carbonate: a hard rock
that barely sustains a tough breed.
Therefore, only one color's allowed
in this town—and that color is red.
Also the way I remember Moscow.

The color of the canyons and dirt.
The color of a hawk's tail, cactus

blooms, or an occasional pickup.
Bullseyes, chili peppers, politics.
And, of course, a football team.

You name it. But most certainly
it is the color of the blood shed
by the ten generations that tried
to carve a living out of this stone.

So that's why she went right out
and bought herself a flashy new
Volcanic Orange MINI Cooper.

Just to let them all stew over it.

TWICE, AT LEAST

~ for Andrea Byers

Two times,
that we know,
she begged him
to put a stop to it...
to call off those missing
links assembled in his name.

Two times, that the committee
investigating him has on record,
she dialed, pled with, her father
for the call to cease and desist.

Two times, she tried to save him
from his own disintegrating mind.

And... the man who twice ignores
his own daughter... the man who
has lied to cover up many crimes,
and then lied to cover up the lies,
and has even asked that daughter
to lie herself, for his sick, dying
cause...
      is a shadow that Hell
      awaits with trembling.

The Richer Fields

~ for Irma Neal, on her 91st birthday

To grow up among those rich fields
in the corner of northeast Oklahoma,
near the Grand Lake o' the Cherokees,
and later on, to live for three decades
just a mile from the old farmhouse
you were born in…

                         to speak of
native soil is not some metaphor,
dirt so close to the color of blood
we couldn't help but tell tales of it.

That's why over 90 journeys around
the sun, in the arms of that land filled
with family above and ancestors below,
leaves a soul with roots that will never
fully come out of such solid ground.

So let us abide now in the power
of good memories, the strength
of the roots that remain with us
here, far away, and in these richer
fields of the eternal stories of home
that will ever have roots of their own.

The Nature of Work

~ for Lou Kohlman

A neighbor who walks
the block twice a day,
says I am the hardest-
working poet that she
has ever seen...
               when
she finds me hunched
over a wheelbarrow or
moving a massive stone
with a refrigerator dolly.

I ask if she's seen others?
She says, *Not that I know of.*

And, I like being seen as hard-
working, because so many people
believe that poets don't work at all.

They don't know what poets do,
really—but work isn't exactly
what they would call it...

they just know *they* work
and get paid money for it.

So when I sweat and groan,
curse and wrestle with stones,
to her I look like I am working.

Labor that breaks backs and bones
has a proud history of appearances.

And this makes me fortunate among
the ranks of poets… who appear
to be doing nothing at a desk
or in a coffee shop all day.

As long as I'm careful
not to explain how
the rocks are just
an alphabet…

and with each
one that I put
in its place…

I'm composing.

ANY *WHO* IN THERE?

> ~ for Lou "Who" Kohlman

If we are, in the end,
simply *who* what we do,

meaning that, what we are
is merely an extension of it,

because we've always worked
there, or we thought working

there was all we'd ever wanted,
what happens to the 'me' in us

when we come home from our
very last day of that dream job?

Who're we supposed to be now?
And, what on earth shall we do

with this losing of our selves?
The job was all we ever were.

And so all they do is give us
a gold watch at the goodbye

party, and then send us home
with a smattering of applause

and more than enough time
on our newly idle hands to

try to find a new *who* to be,
maybe even locate the one,

the better, lifelong *who*,
we have always been.

Like A Snowflake

~ for Jody Karr

After you'd flown back home
from that business in Boston,
she fluttered straight to you.

A snow-white dove... one
with a bloodied wing... one
that had been domesticated
before being thoughtlessly
tossed out in a front yard
by a malfunctioning soul.

You, like a Snow White to
the better souls of animals
that recognize a gift in you.

You, another Betty White...
rescuing them from the low-
down of lesser beings among
the forms of life below heaven.
And, Snowflake was the name
you gave her, and, snow-white

she stayed until her sweet soul
took its flight—a sad-sweet day
in the life of your guardian spirit.

Sinking In

~ for Bishop (2008 – 2021) & Chris & Bill

Such a little giant.
Such a sweet face…
with a big vocabulary…

and if you didn't understand
right away, he would just stare
what he'd meant until it sank in.

Such a cute chocolate mop-head
with short legs and a pink-purple
tongue that meant licky business,

a gingerbread boy who would wag
his entire body… just to make sure
you knew you were happy to be seen.

By him, at least. A wiggle welcome
I will certainly miss. A reminder,
as well, of how I should treat

all the good pups I meet.
And… maybe even…
some people too.

STONE AND FIRE, SUN AND MOON

~ for Tina Baker

I wrenched my back,
and wracked my fingers,
working with stones all day.

They teach me that patience
results in less pain. And that
leverage was what God used
to create the earth—and what
will save me an ambulance ride.

And, when the sun's angle said,
in unison with my back, the day
is done, I built a big fire against
the cold and sat by it swapping
looks between the red flames
and what will be a beautiful
Snow Moon in a week or so.

The fire teaches me how much
can't really last… in the end…
everything burns, eventually,
even tequila on its way down,
so, for now, enjoy the warmth.

The quarter moon reminds me
that whatever waxes, wanes...
so let life and our hopes for it
abide within that parenthesis.

And all of it together, stone
and fire, the sun and moon,
helps me understand better
just how little else matters.

SNAP SNAP

> ~ for Tina Baker,
> and my daughter, Sierra

My daughter
is wrapping up
her 25th year and,
so, is already along
in her journey of, sadly,
discovering the field of work,
the hard business of a paycheck,
is strewn with man-boy jackasses.

And—though I've done no poling
of my own on this—it's my guess
that about 90 to 95% of women
in the workforce just snapped
their fingers and mumbled
something like "Mmhm."

And while I hold no hope
that this subspecies of men
will die off, my daughter has
given me a ray of it to grab onto,
that women are, slowly, shrinking
all those jackasses in relative stature.
Something in the size of extra small
to maybe a XX large insignificance.

Just last night, at the end
of what she hadn't known
would be a last day on a job,
she liberated herself from one,

and popped by my friend's back patio
(where the two of us happened to be
railing against male idiots ourselves,
both of us older now and striving
not to be among those jackasses).

                      And she sat
and joined us in sipping margs, and
our railing against idiots, occasionally
putting us in our own idiot places…

                      And I sat
amazed at her poise and power
when she snapped her fingers
and said, "Welp, anyway,
done with that one."

FREEDOM BATH

~ for Steve Hill

Five months now
in our new home,
and I'm still some-
what a stranger to
certain spaces in it.

I pass by, on my way
through the bathroom
to a big closet, a rather
remarkable tub-jacuzzi-
for-two, that looks to be
intended for other people,
the kind who make money.

My wife very much relishes
lengthy sessions in its luxury,

because she's better at soaking
up, and in, the gifts and pleasant
surprises life sometimes offers us,

while I worry too much about things
like shrinking water tables, questionable
farming practices, and the swelling oceans.

Recently she had the thing humming
with Epsom salt… and I think even
milk and honey… or some such…
and she coaxed me to take it over
when she was done.

                        I thought,
well, she is a very clean person.
So, why not? And I slid on in,
jets massaging my bad back…
soothing my raging Achilles…
that is never not sore as hell…

and I began to float—spiritually,
I mean. My body began to sing out
for more physical justice in its world.
I felt on the verge of tears for this new
wondrous country I had discovered…

and that is when Sir Wallace Williams
welled up deep in my Scottish genes,
and I had the sudden urge to yell:

            "Freedom!"

Thank God I didn't.

Is It Worth Losing Sleep Over?

~ for Anne Roberts

The longer I'm alive
the more the question
becomes: 'Is anything?'

For large chunks of my life
I've been a champion sleep-
loser. I was born with a rest-

less mind. Some, who know me,
might say relentless. Whichever it is,
it is not all that easy to sleep next to.

With a young daughter, losing sleep
became my full-time job. But now
that she's 26, I am reconsidering

even her. Because my mom,
at 90, still loses sleep over
her, and me, and dad...

to the point it has, alas,
metastasized, I fear...
it's what holds her up.

And losing sleep over
a dying Earth does no
earthly good. Because,

if I'm going to fight that
fight, I'll need every ounce
of sleep I ever lost, and more.

So it's embarrassing to admit
I woke up earlier than usual
this morning with this poem

on my mind… I had started
thinking about it last night…
and so, I had trouble sleeping.

Not Fair

> ~ for the children of war

There are things your parents
are busy not telling you about

as they stuff your backpacks
with underwear and socks,

or their suitcases with bras
and citizenship documents.

It's because they have to do with
what happens when kids grow up

and turn into leaders who have
too much power, and money,

and awful toys that hurt others
when they flip switches, or push

bad buttons… meaning, there is
no way to explain madness to you.

Your current understanding of toys
is much better and shouldn't change.

So, choose your favorites, but only
those you can carry for a long time.

You will not understand this either.
But, you need to trust your parents

on this one—we know it's hard…
and we are so sorry about all this.

And we hope, someday, you will
finally understand just what it is

that we are asking you to
forgive us for.

What I Can

~ for the refugees of war

My heart contracts with each new
story I gather from your border
with Poland. My limbic system
sparks and shorts every time
I spot a toddler's Spiderman
backpack bobbing on the puffy
shoulders of a heavy winter coat.

And when that little girl's hands
on the window inside the train
mirrored her father's... there
on the deck outside, because
he was staying to likely die...
I screamed at the television.
A vapid and worthless gesture.

And though it will seem as empty,
like nothing that matters right now,
I am asking you to close your eyes
and begin to remember to always
remember this historical truth...

when the poets and the painters,
the playwrights and bards, those
keepers and tellers of our stories,

choose your side… your ultimate,
if not inevitable, victory has already
taken root, and has begun its spread
all throughout the hard soil and stone
of what eventually becomes known,
without a semblance of doubt,
to future generations.

The Least of These

~ for the animals of war

There's no one at fault
less than you. War being
one of the more immediate
ways we ruin your simple lives.

And no one tallies the number of your
dead… yet another layer of insult…
our neglect knowing no bounds.

So we forget the bombs blow
your feathers out of trees…

incinerate you in the fields
where you graze…
                           horrors
I refuse to illuminate further.

Evidence that some mistakes
were made during the six days
God spent prioritizing creation.

The Reluctant Invader

~ for the Russian soldier

Perhaps you've glanced
out the frost-glazed windows
of your tanks and transport trucks
and caught glimpses of the hunkered
humanity that surrounds you, the insane
proximity of their lives and last names.

Perhaps you were lied to, by a senior
officer—who knew he would have to
to keep your resolve firm and aim true.

Perhaps you are young, and so do not
believe you have any choices... not in
these terrible matters... even though
you know, in places you feel like
you have to keep hidden...

there is a God-sized "No"
lurking beneath your orders.

For Your Consideration

~ for President Volodymyr Zelenskyy

On the outside chance you live,
you'll likely still never see this
bit of advice. But if you do…

and the war is over—not by
having won it, because that
is, already, not possible—

I'll offer this soft suggestion:
Retire. Effective immediately.
It may not make sense at first.

But, you are creating a man-god,
played by a currently beloved actor,
who may very well believe in the role.

And so far the performance is magnificent.
Right down to the biceps and eye-contact.
And your country would not be where it is

without you… not exactly… anyway…
but when this is over, you may find it
very difficult to live up to yourself.

Just ask Odysseus what it's like
to come home to peace time,
a wife staring off into space.

So, your *best* bet for fame
and immortality is: to die,
in an air strike or gun battle.

That is not crude, nor thoughtless,
it is just based on historical precedent.
And yet… one possible option might be

to develop a new character. One filled
with an extraordinary, quite genuine,
and unwavering sense of humility.

OUR REPRESENTATIVES

~ for the dead of war

They say God is with us,
that he watches over us all.
Maybe you're with him now.
Maybe he's had the chance to
explain what happened... why.

If so... I envy you that answer...
though I envy nothing else about
the absurdity, cruelty, inhumanity,
and obsidian injustice of your death.

As far as I'm concerned, Heaven
has as much to answer for here
as any granite-faced dictator...
the latest red-tailed poster child
for Satan having outdone himself.

But... whatever I have to say on this
is quite too late for you. And the only
thing I'm sure of is that more are soon
to follow—an unfortunate condition
of the thundering lunacy that is war,
and the oblivion it's obliged to offer.

Which leaves me with this very little
to offer in the wake—these words
I will ask as many of those still
living as I can to mark…

You… you were us.

And… we will be
you, soon enough,

if we do not stand
against what did this.

This, at Least

> ~ for those far from the war

Realizing what you cannot do,
and the extent to which it is not
your fault, matters. Sitting in front
of some television and holding fast
to frustration over your helplessness
will not help. The human machine
is archaic and so, is not designed
for a news cycle that refreshes
every few minutes. Let it go.
You weren't born in Warsaw.
You cannot volunteer today—
especially if your passport's expired.
So let's begin with breathing. You'd be
useless without this all-important practice.
And it will be critical to any next step—
which might be to tend to your spirit?
It starves, like the body. Maybe make
coffee or tea. Yes, the spirit likes that.
Turn off anything with a battery in it.
The spirit needs that. Face the quiet.
Spirit demands it—nerve-wracking
as it may be… there is something
so crucial on the other side of it.

In Threes

~ for Cheryl Tarter

When there are at least three
things... like horses, music,
and kids... to talk about,

three women... who stand
on three sides of the political
fence... can still find a pasture

big enough to take a daily walk in.
Except Sundays... that day set aside
for the Trinity and the hymns about it,

the best among them in three-quarter
time (the ex-Baptist in me insists).
For it is within holy trinities,

such as these, that we find
solutions to the vast problems
of a world that steadily marches

to four beats per measure, our best
offerings for those generations
coming up behind us.

IT'S TRICKY

> ~ for Brady Peterson

So, here on my 57th birthday,
I find myself talking with the dead.

Don't worry, it's common among poets.
Just ask my friend, Brady… he does it.

And I don't know about him, but,
for me, it is not that I miss them,

as much as it is I find them to be
better conversationalists… slow-

talkers… like I'm a slow-thinker.
Mine is an old processor, bogged

up and down from decades lost to
sifting through useless information.

The dead speak clearly, though briefly,
leaving long stretches to the imagination.

Apparently, one of the perks of shifting
into the spirit realm, is defragmentation.

In other words, the dead get to the point.
There's no need for bombast after the deal

is signed, sealed, and permanently delivered.
A refreshing break from the drone of living.

As for who it is that I am speaking with…
they've requested their names not be used.

Which is just a cheeky way to get around
the honesty that… I'm never quite sure.

One Thing Leads to an Otherwise

~ for Bob Wood

Who do we suppose
was the first one among us
to ever speak on God's behalf?

I'm thinking beyond the Old Testament.

So lightning strikes a little too close to
the entrance of the cave and some
awestruck troglodyte feels led
to say a few words.

                And,
voilà, a new moral code
is given birth, as well as
credence, since the others
have nothing else to go on,

and God leans down, listens in,
rolls his eyes, and quotes the lines
he knows T.S. Eliot will pen someday:

> "That is not it at all,
> That is not what I meant, at all."

But he doesn't say it loud enough

for the endless string of others
who will come to speak for him
to hear and, hopefully, catch on.

And so we now have no drought
of morals, with their hierarchies,
to contend with down here below,
thanks to all who have participated.

Therefore, let us continue on in our
"Contest of Perpetual Concern for
the Depravity of All Who Believe
Otherwise." For… without it…
what else would we have to do?

A Working Title

~ for Shayla Dodge

Near the end of the 1980s…
when President Reagan believed
he brought down the Berlin Wall…
Germans on both sides of its shadow
were able to continue on in the journey
towards their eventual disillusionment
with living in a free market economy.

That's the problem with each next
Grand Metanarrative that comes
down the human superhighway.

> "This should do it.
>   For everyone."

At least until everyone notices
that pink Snuggies and fidget
spinners didn't bring them
the true inner fulfillment
they sought with credit.

More and more we see
that less and less will be
what we get from a small
sphere that gave too freely.

That's why LESS IS MORE
as a green bumper sticker
is not funny anymore…

and why this last will not
be the least of all the great
-isms to form as more than
just the new theoretical wet
dream of last-gasp academics.

Something along the last lines:

> "Find some land that still
> has water underneath it,
> and grow veggies."

Just There

~ for Riha Rothberg

Out of the corner of my eye
is where most of the trouble
starts... those things I could
have done without seeing...

the man with what'll soon be
skin cancer holding up his sign
on the offramp of Mopac, there
in the 103° of what's way too early
in the summer for it... who is either
lying, or isn't, about needing help...

the woman who slaps her child
in a booth at the Subway (where
I've been forced to stop, because,
sometimes, the road offers nothing
else) because he's whining about not
getting the bag of chips he wanted...

the three shining objects in a perfect
line hovering above the Rockies just
south of Colorado Springs on I-25
that, when I glanced down to see
if I was still between the stripes,
weren't there, seconds later...

the green-eyed woman with the reddest
of hair listening in the backest of rows
at my reading in Santa Fe... who later
showed up at the Anasazi bar, where
the stool next to me happened to be
empty.

A Simple Abundance

~ for Karen Zundel

Because of a commitment I made
to Erato—back when I'd visited
Mount Parnassus in a previous
life—my savings account knocks
and sputters like a Ford Model T
trying to cross the Mojave Desert.

So, travel for me is a careful collage
of KIND bars and couches of friends.
I'll hike any trail that doesn't charge
for natural beauty, drive into any
national park that doesn't have
a kiosk with a cash register.

Because of promises made
to both Calliope and Euterpe,
while there on the Mount of Muses,
my wallet usually contains what little
the good George Washington has left
to offer. So, hobbies for me involve
constructing contemporary ruins
out of tequila bottles and deer
bones, charred cedar stumps
and a bottomless quarry
of Texas limestones.

And because the sister
of tragedy, Melpomene,
grabbed me before I got
the hell outta Greecetown,

I've learned to accept poetry's
relative anonymity, even come to
appreciate not being recognized in
the toiletry aisle of the grocery store.

The Lucky Among Us

~ for Chelsea Kaye Major

It's the moment we discover
the money they'd promised us
from the job that the education
promised us, the one that society
promised would be the culmination
of the pursuit of our happiness that
the Constitution had promised us,
isn't cutting the spiritual mustard.

That's when the lucky among us
look up at the big revolving door
that spins us into Goldman Sachs
and say to our hardworking selves
"What in the hell was I thinking?"

Then—before we think too much,
or have time to talk our new selves
out of it—we find that reborn self
selling books in a mobile pop-up
store out on some street corner
in a town like Meridian, Idaho.

BROTHER, FATHER, FRIEND

~ for Bill Shope, from Terri Stubblefield

When dad left
and she was only
two, you, much older,
had to become a father.

When she married, and you
decided that Joe was a decent
enough man, you became like
the brother you never got to be.

And when the good husband died,
you became a father again… and yet
remained a brother too, since by now
you had had all that practice being both.

So, now that trouble has come your way,
she's here to take her turn: sister, mother,
friend. A loved one who remembers being
loved so abundantly, there's plenty to share.

Who Else

~ for Jody Karr

You get one call, she said,
from the confines of being
yet alive, to one who's passed
on into that ultimate freedom.

And, I did not come to this table
with my choice in mind, one made
ahead of time, it seems I should say.
I wanted the poem to surprise us both.

And what surprises me first is how fast
I let go of the need for it to be a human.
I have talked with many of those in life,
and so, I have no reason to believe they

would be more interesting in the after.
No, I want to hear from one who had
no voice while here amid the problems
of physical bodies in this harsh world.

So, I choose Cayenne, sweetest dog
I've loved. Because, certainly, now
she would be able to speak to me.
A thing I just know in my bones.

I would ask for the secret to life,
because I sensed that she knew it.
And I would ask about those days,
at the very end, when she began to

look through walls, doors, and trees,
into something much more than what
was merely on the other side of them.
I stood beside her, but couldn't see it.

And then, I would say please help me
understand your mother a little better.
You two had something that we don't.
(And, I won't say I'm jealous? but…).

Look, whether she answers any of my
questions or not, the bottom line here
is that I couldn't think of anyone else
I'd rather listen to for a few hours.

A Good Choice

~ for Betty & Tommy Potts,
from Carole Moody

What's happened
in the church kitchen
has stayed in the church
kitchen, since before Vegas
was a twinkle in the desert's eye.

Friends are made of those bubbling
pots, and greasy sheet pans, sliding in
and out of long-used, well-loved ovens.

Ask any pastor who's ever listened through
the walls... the jokes are a hell of a lot
dirtier over that sink. And besides,
the pastor's told a few herself
while helping out in there.

When the friend comes
with a husband, he often
becomes that hilarious big
brother you had never had...

the one who teases relentlessly,
but yet helps out anytime you ask.

The one who stays out of the kitchen,
unless he is needed. The one who is
out in the church gardens telling
dirty jokes of his own, whether
to a buddy, or the butterflies,
or some alien friend he made
from a remote viewing session.

It's crazy crafts for supper club…
it's Palak Paneer and Carrot Halwa
for the Diwali celebration. Or the pig
roasted on the church grounds for that
South Sea themed dinner one night…

yes… they are the family we choose.

The Job

~ for Jeanne Fell

You asked how I have changed
in the cocoon of this pandemic.

And there's another way in which
(for better, or worse... depending
on who you give a chance to speak)
I walk back into the light of a fresh
and different day. And it's as simple
as it is trouble for the pocketbook:

> An exponential resolve.
> A more profound belief
> in the power and necessity
> of poetry to heal a wounded,
> wayward, battle-weary world.

As we emerge, rub our eyes,
and sigh in the face of yet
another rise in cases...

and realize no amount
of yoga-meditation classes,
and self-help books, can cure
the 21st century of one sick mind
determined to destroy another culture,

and then try not to think too much
about the mercurial mixing of
wildfires with high winds,
or high pressure domes,

we pause... look around...

then wonder where we will turn
for solace, and maybe a tip on where
to place the next foot, since just standing
around for the rest of the century is not
an option for those with children
and a working conscience.

Look, it's not sad
that the poets are at
their best in apocalypses.
It's merely that thing they do.
They hear the news, what little of it
they can bear. They read the times, painful
as they may be. They observe the behaviors
of others in gas stations and grocery stores,

and they go home, sharpen their axes
and knives, put on the soundtrack
to *Rocky*, then don uniforms
and get back to work.

HERE, WHERE...

~ for Santa Fe

...people who've not been here before
walk up and squint over their glasses at the
menu on the sidewalk in front of The Shed
and mumble *Well, this looks okay, I guess...*
and then seem shocked when a hostess tells
them it will be an hour wait for a table on
the patio because, *it's like, 1:30 on a Tuesday
afternoon in mid-May*, they say to themselves.

...a divorcée-turned-artist who's lived here
all of a year or so, curses out the window of
her Subaru at the California tag that's not
turning left on a yellow light at the corner
of Old Santa Fe Trail and Paseo de Peralta.

...Navajos selling jewelry in the walkway of
the Palace of the Governors are still
wearing surgical masks, because this is not
their first time around the block with the
way a viral devastation makes its way across
the sea.

...some very large white man with very
large white hair sticking out from under a
very large white cowboy hat always seems

to be sitting in a very small stool at the very end of every very small bar in this small town.

...the colors of turquoise and mud brown go together like blue poetry and red wine.

...the marriage of the red chile sauce with the green chile sauce ends in a hot orgasm of gastronomical consummation.

...those with means often have to step over those without it, on the hard edges along West San Francisco Street.

...teenagers visiting from the Midwest eat at Taco Bell, because they think that crap qualifies as Mexican food.

...New Mexican cuisine is as unlike Mexican as Texas barbecue is from something you might get in New York that wants to go by the same name.

...the good people who wash your dishes and work on the line in the kitchen can't afford to eat at the restaurant where they work, let alone live in this movie-star town.

...the gray-haired Apache, in a ragged ballcap with John Lennon glasses, who is waiting for his americano by the wall in the coffee shop, sings along inaudibly to Bob Dylan's "Isis" without missing one word of the thirteen verses as they float out of the ceiling speakers.

...women of a certain age come to live without the men they'd put up with for far too long... as well as more comfortably within their bodies and new lives.

...men of a certain age come to try on new clothes and personalities, because they'd hated their jobs, and the lies and the wives that went with them.

...lowriders pound the dirty pavement of the plaza, because the young and restless natives want to remind all the white legs poking out of cargo shorts who was here first.

IMITATING ART

~ for Sandra Harrington

If my good wife ever lets me go,
for her sake and good reasons,
I'll find myself living the lines
of one of her all-time favorite
Garth Brooks songs—which,
for the record, it should be said,
was composed by Tony Arata—
where I would all of a sudden be
looking back, on the memory of
the love we'd shared for the years
we had when all the world was right.
And it's true I'll be glad I didn't know
the way it all would end or would go.
Because it's also painfully true that
our lives are better left to chance.
Oh Tony, you with the beautifully
sad words. Oh Garth… you with
your heartbreaking performances.
You both knew I could've missed
the pain, but the problem, the one
that's always been, and will be,
is that I would have had
to miss the dance.

This Dance

~ for Sandra Harrington

The easier thing would've been
not to have a daughter, I suppose.
They are such complicated creatures.
Wonderfully complicated, I should say.
Especially in the years that end in -teen,
and when it comes to the boys they can't
understand. Which we understand why.
Then come the car wrecks, both literal
and otherwise, problematic relationships
with problematic men and troubling jobs
with other troubling men as their bosses.

Like I said, there are much easier things.
But, then, what would we have done,
who would we have been and what
would we have become, without
the wonder and awe of them.
That sensation that stirs
the simmering soup
of our souls each
time we peer
into those
blazing
eyes.

Allways

> ~ for the LGBTQQIP2SAA community
> (lesbian, gay, bisexual, transgender, questioning,
> queer, intersex, pansexual, two-spirit (2S),
> androgynous, and asexual)

I secretly thrill
to a beautiful and
growing array of new
variations on the human
theme I see walking about
among the more predictable,

softly erasing old anthropology
and the ancient troubles carved
from the binary stones of female
and male, wondrous beings strutting
fresh sets of bones in noncommitment
to any of the recent rages in fashion…

setting the stage for some new age
that will have a new name ending
in -ism, one that represents a sliding
scale on the DNA threads of a species,
an exploding number of kaleidoscopic
choices within the infinitudes of love.

An Elevated Soul

> ~ in memory of Judith Mulliken Dippo
> (1934 to 2022)

Being born on the eastern shore
of the Hudson, in Dobbs Ferry,
and then nurtured in the throes
of World War II and the Great
Depression are good ingredients
for a spirited and vigorous soul,

a soul expanded all the more by
a youth spent up in Silverton…
hidden below the fabulous peaks
of Colorado's San Juan Mountains,
with its movie sets, stars, hair-raising
train rides, and its blazing snowstorms.

A time when an industrious soul learned
to bake and sew, and to grow vegetables,
to can peaches in the dog days of August.
All those brownies, pies, and prom dresses,
the banana bread, the Halloween costumes.
(Because the world and Walmart were not
going to wrap it all up in plastic for you.)

An age when the power and pleasure
of a good book was still a given…

the importance and beauty of it
as palpable as the blossoms
on geraniums, or the little
crowns in a sea of marigolds.

Yes, this is how we chart the course
of a lovely soul in a journey well spent.

Striking out from the humble shoreline
at sea level, traveling up the numberless
trails and byways that weave the world,

then coming to rest at the 11,018 feet
at the pinnacle of Red Mountain Pass,
on a Million Dollar Highway to the sky.

WE NEVER KNOW

~ for Sam and Cathey Lanham

I don't know what it was
at the particular time...

my parents unhappy
in the new apartment
they were not adjusting
to—the big lie they label as
independent living these days...

or maybe the wet dreams of another
dictator blowing up children and their
pets in the happier country next door
in order to ward off the memories
of a silent and brutal father...

or maybe it was a marriage
wincing in the throes of
a big move to a bigger
place just up the road
in the middle of a big
pandemic, that had me
off the road and hanging
around that place too much,

but... I wasn't doing well...

the night you took the time
to send me a text from a birthday
dinner in Las Vegas, New Mexico…

and tell me you two were reminiscing
about a different birthday… last fall…

one where I'd been present, and we
partied a little too late, and drank
a bit too much, while we talked
long into the night about life
and poetry, and more life,
and then you ended with

We love you, dear friend.

And I answered with

My God, I needed this
message tonight…
thank you…
so much.

If It Weren't Too Late

> ~ in memory of Teddi Burleson
> February 6, 1965 to May 9, 2022

You were the first friend
I ever made, that I can recall.
And I've never been good at it.

Just like I've never been any good
at maintaining one, many would say.
Including you… if it weren't too late.

But you were true, over the decades,
despite my shortcomings, following
my odd endeavors from the edges
of a responsible American fantasy.
You'd still be, if it weren't too late.

My earliest memories, from year five
for us, center on the swimming pool
out at your house that, way back then,
I'd thought was "out in the country."

And, for some reason, horse apples,
which I did not know, until now,

have a more poetic name…
the "Osage orange"…

which I would've
told you about—if
it were not too late...
but, if it weren't too late,
I wouldn't have looked it up.

And my God, those garage bands
in our teens. Me on my candy apple
red electric guitar trying to eke out
that lead break on Pat Benatar's
"Hit Me with Your Best Shot,"
or that blazing synthesizer solo
on Scandal's "Goodbye to You."

Which, if it weren't too late...
I would tell you, you sang straight
from the gut, for damn good reasons
I didn't find out about until later in life.

And so it is, if it were not too late,
I would also want to say thanks.
Thank you for being a better
friend than I was to you.

And I'd say I'm sorry
as well... if only...

THE HISTORY OF A HUG

~ for Cheryl Tischer

I have never liked them,
except under strict circumstances.
Something in my ancient Germanic genes.
Something in those old English roots—

chiefly Cornish—that gut-level tug
of a homeland my mother never
needed a DNA test to feel—

a stormy and seafaring folk
who used it as a squeezing
grip in wrestling, a rough
grasp with the arms, or
the unwanted advances
and embrace of a bear.

Though the Swedes
said that it qualified
as comfort, affection,
a form of consolation,

those chilly Norwegians
gave what's called a *hugge*,
back in the days of Valhalla,
Odin's huge hall of the fallen.

Even the word itself requires
an exaggerated, uncomfortable
scrunching of the lips together.

Picture a couple of ol' Vikings
slamming fists on their backs
after a big and bloody battle.

So… as you can see now…
the reason for my aversion
is as etymological as it is
biological or… say…
pathological.

What Time We Have

~ for Eliza Jane,
from her great-grandmother DuAnne Redus

Should we call it a defect
when a little heart is just
too full of light and love
to go on beating beyond
the eleven months given?

Should we say a thing like
Taken from us? when some
angels are simply so above
our 'having' to begin with?

Could we say, instead, that
we've been graced with this
sacred seed of some distant
star that burned too brightly
for our world to comprehend?

And for the time we spent here
in her presence… would we not
admit that our own hearts grew
to the size of Georgia… until
they broke open and spilled
the celestial light she filled
our waning spirits with?

Because It Has to Be Said

~ for Americans with wombs

This morning, the highest court we have
ruled that lead bullets and bump stocks
are more important than your bodies
and birthright to self-determination.

Once again, good Christian soldiers
have redetermined God's priorities...
in the absence of any direct commands
from the Lord of the Universe. Heaven's
silences have always made crazed zealots
terribly fidgety and nervous in the lurch.

But hell, I'm just a smug and privileged
white man, like honorable judges Brett
Kavanaugh and ol' Clarence Thomas—
despite his skin. So what would I know?

Yet, as a father of an empowered daughter,
husband of a bread-winning wife, and a son
of the best of mothers, I know at least this:
Where I stand, what I will fight for... and
which gender brings to life such beauty,
as well as the only genuine hope for
any amount of tomorrows.

#4305

~ for Cynthia "Boo" Beath

for #,
4 is a sound
integer, the points
on the cross I grew up
worrying about, a carpenter
made legend by the bloody holes
in his wrists and bare feet on the day
religion got its head twisted backwards
yet again—a habit it has never broken.

3 goes quite well with my penchant for
odd numbers—the number of stripes
on my right arm—the sharp, curved
arms of a triskelion carved in my left.
Fire, water, stone. Faith, hope, love.
Life, death, rebirth. Past, present,
future. Creation, preservation, and
destruction. God unable to make up
his mind about what form to take.

Zero is the least complicated…
for me, at least. "Nothing from
nothing leaves nothing," if you
ask the key-bustin' Billy Preston.

It's how we come in,
then how we go out…
so, it is the final balance.

5's too much, if you ask me.
Well, except maybe, possibly,
when it comes to wonders like
fingers, and toes. Sight, sound,
smell, taste, and touch. Or, say,
the great lakes, the Marx brothers,
and let's not forget the Spice Girls.

Altogether, if we look at the letters on
a phone dial (and make the zero wild)
we have the rather ominous hashtag:

#HELL…

or #HECK, for Baptists

Or… it might simply
be the gate code
for paradise.

BRINGING IT BACK

~ for Danna Primm

After a 20-year ban,
the political intelligentsia
of my homeland want to bring
back the sport, they say, of cocks
ripping each other to shreds using
genetically-tuned beaks and talons.
(With maybe a few razor blades
tied to legs for good measure?)
So, better start choosing your
Roundheads and Whitehackles
soon... They'll go like hotcakes.

And they are hoping that the word,
sport, will help cover their deadly sins.
These mostly white farts with money.

And yet I say, "Why stop with cocks?"
History offers us a plethora of options.
I mean, how exciting would it be, once
again, to watch lions maul and devour
Christians in our colossally converted
football stadiums, underneath those
night-defying, near-blinding lights?

Finding Peace

~ for Terry Clark

Alone,
I go to the stones…
because stones know alone.

Those saints of a lithoid silence,
their prayers one long eternal sigh
over the relentless hum and buzz
of humans laboring under a hot
illusion of progress, conquest,
and the suffering that follows.

I keep my ears ever peeled…
as I form them into igneous altars
and tribunals of fire. But they never
speak. Neither in protest, nor praise.

Thus, the perfect Council of Elders…
a cloistered cairn of monks and sages
who teach by emanation the ultimate
peace to be made:
            That alone…
is not such a bad place to be.
And so there is no need
to fear it as a place
to end up.

I Know It Seems

> ~ for Christopher Everett

It seems like nothing, what we do, waking,
stretching, making coffee as if God were
grading our technique.

It seems like nothing, carefully checking
out angles of morning light, or degrees of
cloud cover, gauging the temperature, to
determine where we will position ourselves
to begin a day's process.

It seems like nothing, what we do, when
first, we read poetry before we begin,
scratching notes in margins between sips,
consulting a dictionary on some sexy word
we cannot believe we've never heard of.

It seems like nothing, lighting a candle to
set the Muses on fire, then observing the
work habits of a chipmunk in the bushes,
as we contemplate the nature of metaphor
and impression.

It seems like nothing, what we do, pausing,
as long as need be, over the blank page, or
canvas, before committing that first mark.

It seems like nothing, jumping up, mid-thought, to run find the book that has that end-all line in it we need for the problem at hand, writing it out on a paper scrap to tape to the wall above us, a guide for the rest of the day.

It seems like nothing, what we do, going for long walks on late mornings and afternoons, collecting hyssop to boil in simple syrup for the gin and tonics sure to come... and yet pausing first to weep over the impossible emerald velvet of rows of head-high corn, strutting through late July, as if the world might just depend on it.

It seems like nothing, cooking dinner as slowly as possible, talking into the sunset over what came and passed since waking, cocktail glasses dangling... then stepping into the trees to join a church of fireflies.

Yes, it seems like nothing, what we do.

PSALM 151

~ for Sam and Cathey Lanham

O Father of the Flood...
   God of Ten Plagues...

O Sender of Bears to murder
   42 teenagers, for making fun
      of Elisha's big ol' bald head...

O Mighty Interior Designer of the world...
   Chief Meddler in the affairs of men...

I call upon you now! The whole damn
place needs redecorating. All the guns
you supplied your followers are now
aimed at their decent neighbors, yea,
whose blood runs in the sewer pipes
of the formerly mundane suburbs,
while criminally insane resort-
dwellers cheer them on.

O Lord of Lamentations...

deliver us from the madness
and the bias of the High Court
that slams a gavel in your name!

O Torturer of Poor Job...

there are those up in the loftiest
seats of this forlorn land who need
to swim with the fishes of the Red Sea,
like the minions of Pharoah in Exodus...

but I can't do it, for I am a law-abiding
citizen. I mean, you used to take care
of these things in the Old Testament.

Please, dear God! I will praise you
    with tambourine and dancing,
        with strings and the flute,
           and clash of cymbals.

           Praise the Lord.

Psalm 152

> ~ for Cathey and Sam Lanham

O Lord of Leviticus,
    Lover of Lists
        and Numbers,

O God of Deuteronomy,
    Lover of Laws and
        Blood Sacrifice,

if you are as nosy and all
up in our business—how I
define "omnipresence"—as
the churchgoers I grew up
avoiding want to believe,

then you're well aware of
those who dwell among us
that are uselessly occupying
valuable space and breathing
precious air in our atmosphere.

They are the devout disciples of
the overly powerful and truly evil
among us who corporately occupy
space and knowingly destroy the air
we try to keep on breathing, because

we have no choice… you know…
the present-day Ahabs and Herods.

So, if you need a bit of help creating
a modern list of sinners who deserve
to be plagued by fiery hail and frogs,
turned into pillars of salt, or maybe
placed on an altar, to be a fragrant
sacrifice, one that's pleasing unto
your holy and heavenly nostrils,

please… just let me know.

Son of a Bundy

~ for Ammon Bundy,
the future of this country, if we don't wake up

I get it, friend.
That deep longing
for the simpler days.
The times when a dude
done us wrong, we kil't'im.

Hell, I would give anything too
if the Dutton Ranch wasn't just
the set of a wildly popular series
from Paramount. Millions agree.

Let's bring back Lorne Greene
as Ben Cartwright on *Bonanza*.
I mean, who didn't love Hoss…
a man the size of a prairie schooner
on the back of a thoroughbred named
Chub… a horse who outlived him.

Besides, you've got the beard,
the big hat and that mountain
of rage for suits and soft men
who hide behind crooked laws
and evil government regulations
to severely pull this thing off…

the way you parade your bad ass
into high school gyms and small
townhall meetings to intimidate
abiding and cowering villagers.

You're like that actor in westerns,
the one no one knows the name of,
because he always plays the S.O.B.
or maybe the S.O.B.'s sidekick...
all weaselly and greasy in black.

But son? y'ain't never gonna be
no Rip Wheeler, Dutton's right
hand, and the chief enforcer.
Because, when Hollywood
and the Wild West meet,
they drink too much
and tell big lies.

Yes, you will...
    eventually...
get over yourself.

Even if it takes death
to come do it for you.

Modus Operandi

~ for Danna Primm

The-Little-Virus-That-Could
set that world of acronyms
on fire. From the beginning
we knew that "Coronavirus
Disease of 2019" would have
to be shortened to something.

And, while for some time HITH
stood for Hospital In The Home,
or, for some, How In The Hell…

for her it came to be understood
as Hide In The House. And she
did have good reasons. Reasons
that are not everyone's business.

Groceries had to be figured out,
among other problems to solve.

But, before long, a soft rhythm
set in. Her musicians brought
the church of good harmony
in on a live stream of songs,
6-strings, and familiar voices.

Oh, and also, there was this one
crazy poet she never gave up on.

That wild clan of troubadours,
a family, of sorts, paid regular
visits, and we all crawled our
wily ways through somehow.

And so it is, it turns out,
desperation is the true
mother of invention.

For Grace and Baby Courage

> ~ for Grace, on her 1st birthday,
> from Jeanne "Mimi" Eek

When they come in heavenly teams,
we name them a Host of Angels...
sometimes a Choir, or Chorus.

But, you have been graced
with a courageous Clan...
a closer Family of Angels.

Grandma Donna, leading
the village, will watch out
for you and your mom...

Great-granddad's there
to keep his Army eyes
on you and your dad...

and Uncle Lauris, with whom
you will forever share a birthday,
will be there, as he was, for you all.

So, hold them close to your heart,
just like you do your spirit-pride
of stuffed lions... Courage...

that furry little angel that rode
with Nana through rough days
on the ruby backs of rainbows,

and now... Baby Courage...
for this band of good souls
will surely hold fast to you.

Such blessing, such love,
for you we should call it

    a Grace of Angels.

CRUCIAL

~ for Terry Clark

How different
being alone is
from feeling
lonely.
     Now,
in my late 50s,
I'm mostly alone.
In my teens and 20s,
I was lonely—and a bit
in love with it.
     Loneliness
felt luxurious, and, I thought,
carried a sort of noble mystique.

When, in all truth, it was just easier
than asking Jenny Bentz out, or a few
years later telling the one older, and
married, woman I will wait forever.

Lonely's believing you don't want
to be alone anymore.
     Truly alone,
and beautifully so, is figuring out
you have been sufficient all along.

And now that I've been a solo act,
on the road for decades, anywhere
I park my crew of one, for coffee
or a taco, I can spot the two from
twenty paces.
                    I lift the toasty mug
for a sip and note that he, over in
the corner at 8:00 a.m., is lonely.

I glance down the bar, just past
the salted rim of my glass, and
I see that she's alone, and quite
fine with keeping it that way—
any questions?

                    So, I raise
either glass in my hopeful
toast to all with a decent
chance of getting to it…

may we come to discover
the magnificent difference.

Nicely Done

> ~ for Olivia Julianna, women's rights activist
> who kicked congressman Matt Gaetz's ass

You took on a tiny mind,
because the media gave you
no choice. And you did it with
such a calm, long-suffering voice,
a tone beyond your nineteen years.
You guarded well what you must
have felt and turned your smile,
along with his brutal idiocy,
into almost two million
dollars for the bodies
and rights of women.
I'm holding back as well.
Maybe since we both know
he's just a twelve-year-old boy
trapped behind that square face
of a middle-aged demon who still
loves a round of Beer Pong at night
in the basement of his old frat house.
And some flaccid battle-axes are not,
nor will they ever be, worth fighting.
So just stick with your hard-earned
composure, and surprising grace
under pressure, because both
look beautiful on you.

Of the American Dream

> ~ for congressman Matt Gaetz,
> who got the ass-kickin'

You are Florida's representative
of the odious dung, the sodden
scat—yes, you're the fallacious
feces of the American Dream.

As proteins become the essential
building blocks of its democracy,
vitamins are then absorbed into
the bloodstream, and minerals
are metabolized into its cells…

you're nothing but the pathetic
little pellets, dropped and dried
on the ground beneath its feet.

DENOUEMENT

>Thursday – September 1, 2022

A bizarre twist?
Or a predictable turn?
Could you help me decide?

As I near the last page in the most
anomalous chapter of my odd-to-begin-
with career—that resulted in five books—
why wouldn't I—precisely 30 months in—

on the 1st of September—be jarred awake
at 5:19 a.m., by the text announcing that
the result to my PCR test was positive?

For two and a full-half years I have
evaded that little airborne beast.
But, Covid is a lonely hunter,
and my wet nose is the only
thing running from it now.

Lo, I have become a statistic…
unable to elude the joyful ignorance…
the ecstatic arrogance, of the poppycocked
ignoramuses who could've done their due
diligence and saved many hundreds
of thousands the damn trouble.

Alas, it is tea and toast for me, here
in the low-grade valley of the dark and
feverish shadow of their careless making.

And yet I would not trade this wild season
for all the Barbecue and T-bones in Texas,

nor all the good souls who've joined me
around the fires, stones, and poems
along this Willy Wonka journey.

    May we all emerge.

Good Mister Secretary

~ for Ryan Walters
Oklahoma Secretary of Education

Dear Mr. Walters,

In light of recent events leading to the subsequent firing of a Norman High School English teacher, whom you publicly shamed by name in your missive on state letterhead, I am asking the Oklahoma State Board of Education to regain its soul and revoke your license to bulldoze the sacred arts of learning and enlightenment back over a thousand years to some Medieval junkyard.

Art and literature are beams of light that have guided human civilization through its darkest ages since we first started painting animals and leaving our handprints on cave walls many tens of thousands of years ago.

And all through those ages, attempts to control, ban, squelch, or even destroy them have failed. Turns out artists are a scrappy and relentless brood who've never given up or given in to the likes of you. So do you actually believe you're going to be some kind of exception?

You say there is no place for a teacher with "a liberal political agenda in the classroom." Well sir, I have done time in English departments, as a student and teacher, for almost as long as you have been alive, and I am telling you, I have not met an English teacher without some agenda. But it usually has something to do with a passion for awakening young minds to the beauty of art and great literature, and the power they have to transform our lives for the better.

You say she provided "access to banned and pornographic materials" to her students. My guess would be, then, you must not spend much time on the Internet? Well, just know, those students do. And most of them already know what you're afraid of them finding out.

And one more guess I will make is that, when people like you do things like this, it tends to make young people do the exact opposite of what you so desperately want. Young people are notoriously like that.

A quick example. When I, as a teacher, assigned books for a course at the University of Oklahoma, I found over the more than two decades I taught, that, at an ever-accelerating rate, students tended not to read them. They know how to get around it, and the Internet supplies them a plethora of means. The reason? I was "making" them do it. And the average American student, more and more, as I said, was not going to tolerate such audacity on my part.

So, what have you accomplished here, by firing this young accredited teacher with an agenda? Two things.

The first is: *Nothing*. At least where the good kids you're most worried about, the ones who go to church and promise to vote for you when they're old enough, are concerned. Those kids were not going to read the books she was *not* assigning, mind you—merely supplying access to—anyway.

And the second is: *The best thing*. Because, the bad kids, who I'd bet you're less worried about, since they're never going to vote for you (though you won't admit that), who were not going to read those books

either, because the teacher "suggested"
them, are damn well going to read those
books now. And for no other reason than
your trying to keep them from it. Because
that is what we bad kids live for.

Look, all you had to do to avoid this age-
old predicament, was actually read the
books your history professors assigned you
in college. I'm assuming you went?
Although, when it comes to qualifications
these days?

Anyway, I'm just saying you could have
saved yourself from the harsh way the
history books are now going to remember
you. If they bother.

So, Mr. Walters, you can challenge books,
you can ban them, you can even burn
them, if you are indeed brave enough to
dance with the likes of Hitler.

But we will just keep writing them.
And they will just keep reading them.

Yours duly,
Nathan Brown, Ph.D.
former Poet Laureate of Oklahoma

The Night

> ~ for the wedding
> of Hunter and Dee Hoelscher

Whenever two people meet
in the foothills somewhere,
you know they at least have
a chance. But, the foothills
of Nevada City, California,
in the shadow of the High
Sierras, are special ones.

And if those two people
are introduced by mutual
friends at the town saloon
where they have the best live
music, you're off and running.

But, if the saloon just happens
to be named the Crazy Horse?
Well folks, then it's lights out.

None of that holds a candle,
though, to the grace in the way
that spark is met with a patience,
when one of those two isn't quite
ready for any big commitment yet—
needing to honor a promise to herself.

So, for six months, likely long ones
for him, it's the reach-outs and the
check-ins, along with all of those
no-pressures and frequent run-
ins down at the Crazy Horse,
until there comes that night.

The one when she finally
moves in and lays that
big kiss on his lips...

yes, that's always,
and always will
be, the night.

LEGACY

> ~ for Jymmie and G.K. Stanton

I have seen bitterness handed down
from generation to bitter generation,
like acid eating through the bottom
of a bucket then through the shelf,
then even through the floor itself.

Fussbudgets, so genetically pre-
disposed, there is no knowing
in the bones of another way.

What too many fathers have
left to too many of their sons
may explain the homicide rates
of the world's wealthiest nations,
why governments cannot function,
and why polar ice caps are melting.

That's why the sons and daughters
who were bequeathed the utter
opposites stand so confused
out in the burning streets.

And of course, as God and
biochemistry would have it…
there are the opposites to those

opposites—the better sons of bad
fathers—the broken daughters of
mothers who'd given it their best.

But, what we pass along to the ones
we leave behind must matter somehow.

Else the awful question: Does anything?

And to My Daughter

~ for Jymmie and G.K. Stanton

If it happens I live
another 30 years 'r so,
I will leave to you some
20,000 poems and one
likely unfinished novel.

And I'm already sorry for
how much money you will
not receive from all that.

I never understood
the real meaning
of Net Worth.

So, I'm afraid
my theoretical
executor, were
I able to afford
one, would just
read a short list
of the intangibles
I have to offer you:

The life I tried my best
not to live under the big

bloody paw of the manic
modern machine, damn
the consequences.
                And yes,
there were in the end, a lot.

A dream that art can survive
having been assaulted by mass
production, the ever-presence of
noise and the vacuum of the virtual.

A hope for the human species…
that we will be able to hunch on
down and find those bootstraps.

A love for you that you can wear
like a tattoo into the remaining
days of your life, with all your
daring dreams and holy hopes.

And, as long as the poor thing
is not destroyed by the harsh
truth of the road and stage,
I will leave to you as well,
one magnificent guitar.

Not Just Any Hat

~ for Dorothy Alexander,
requested by Terry Clark

That red fedora never signified
an interest in holding a tea party
for bored, or boring, housewives
stuck in bad or sexless marriages.
Not hers... hers was a picket line.
Hers was meant to take back that
good color from the Republicans
who'd never deserved it anyway.
And if you did not know at first,
when you came to the open mic,
where she stood on that—and
other things—you damn well
did once she took the stage.

Her red fedora was a bright
whetstone keeping her mind
sharp up to the last minute.
It was a battle cry... a call
to fellow citizens to stop
turning their blind eyes.
It was the flag she flew,
the one she carried into
that never-ending war
for humanity's soul.

A Case of You

~ for my guitar

No matter how much I wanted
to believe it was my sad lyrics…
it was you who made them weep.
The poet's never stood a chance
against the vibrating gut of such
a finely-grained and tuned body
made of black walnut and spruce.

Add to that the brooding dignity
of a good mate who's never once
spoken, unless spoken to first…
what better friend has ever been.

And while 6 strings and 20 frets
equals only 120 notes, the two
of us have ridden the crests
of a million soundwaves.

Even when an audience
is small, you never give
anything but your best.
You… my only sister.
To you I sing my song
of simple praise, an ode
to the good you've done.

Fire in the Blood

~ for Siosi'ana Kaufusi,
in honor of one of the world's newest islands:
Hunga-Tonga-Hunga Ha'apai

Oh Moana,
maker of waves,

creator of caves along
the earth's rocky shorelines,

fertile mother of the dark islands
and black stone mountains, raging
with a pelagic mouth full of pearls,

after your long laboring in the dim
volcanic bed of that churning sea,
contractions in the quaking crust,

you give birth to yet another child
in the South Pacific's eternal blue,

a maternal plume, spewing upward
far enough to reach the mesosphere,
your hot tears of lava raining down,

your primal screams that echo…
outward in a torrent of tsunamis.

And here in the steaming after,
we see that you are still angry
with us, oh goddess-mother,
boiling beneath the surface,

with all the petty bickering
over our divisions of land…
as we now destroy our home,
while fighting over pieces of it.

Corinthians Chapter 13
for the Darker Soul

~ for Larry Smith

[4]Death is patient enough, I suppose. Death may even be kind, depending on timing, and the need. It does not envy, for what does it lack? It does not boast, for it has won. It is not proud, it just has a job to do. One it has done for billions of years, and, therefore, does it well.

[5]It is not rude... merely efficient. It is not self-seeking, because it has nothing to gain. Nor lose, for that matter. It is not easily angered, because it is the ultimate source of fear—and so, anger itself—among the living. It keeps no record of wrongs, for it tired of that business eons ago.

[6]Death does not delight in evil, for it is the ending of all vice and virtue alike, but rejoices with the truth, because it plays a fundamental role in the final unraveling of truth's eternal plot.

[7]It always protects, as it is a haven of its own sort. It always trusts there is no way

around its mandate. It always hopes
western culture will give up its futile efforts
to overcome it. And it always perseveres...

yes...

[8]Death never fails. Ever. For where there
are prophecies, they will cease; where there
are tongues, they will be stilled; where there
is knowledge, it will pass away.

As You Say Grace

~ for those without
Tuesday, November 22

As you drive to the scene
of that big dinner this year...
someone with a rundown heart
will be transported by ambulance
to a cup of Jell-O on a hospital tray.

As you light the candles on the set
dining room table... another
will stand in the street
and watch firemen
put out their lives.

As you bake the green
bean casserole with crispy
onions sprinkled over the top...
a shivering woman will pop the lid
off a can of pintos, and eat them cold
beneath the concrete beams of a bridge.

As you slip the dog his piece of turkey
under the table... a soon-to-be stray
will be dumped in a fenceless field
somewhere ten miles out of town.

As you sink an overstuffed
body and satisfied soul
into bed... someone
will be asked to pack
and get out; it's over.

So, as you say grace,
or offer a blessing, or
a prayer, if you have one,
on Thanksgiving this year,

send a little something their
way. A word... or whatever
you've got... and can afford.

To You Who Does Not Like that I Write in the First Person Point of View

I
confess,
yes… that I
do indeed write
confessional poetry…
and prose for that matter.

I have also been told by those
who know better than I, that my
poetry's mostly poorly-written prose.

But to you who does not care for my "I,"
I will say that I write from my perspective
because "I" is who and what I know best.

You, on the other hand, are you, and you
know you better than I. So, for me
to write about you from your
perspective would thus be,
not only second person,
but also riddled with
inaccuracies… not
to mention my new
biases towards you…
if *you* know what *I* mean.

That said, there is one point
of view that I despise more
than any other—and that is
the point of view of a certain
he or a she who writes poetry
in the third person, when clearly
that he or she is damn well talking
about his own… or her own… self.

That industry, it reeks of dishonesty,
and, therefore, will never be for me.

What Gives Us Away

~ for Karen Zundel

As often as not…
it's a t-shirt we choose
to pack and trot out in some
distant country without a clue…

like the time I stood to take my lunch tray
to the kitchen on the western shore of
the Dead Sea… just north of where
Lot's wife had turned to a pillar
of salt… and I spun around
to a bright orange back
proclaiming:

> "Stillwater's Jumpin'
> Little Juke Joint"

She didn't need to face me.
I knew what the front said:

> Eskimo Joe's
> Stillwater, OK

or like
that time
you looked up

from your apple strudel
and the glassy bottom
of a Stiegl Goldbräu
in Innsbruck, Austria

to see the Black and Gold
of your long belovéd homeland
Pittsburgh Pirates parade through
the restaurant and, after passing,

reveal 'Clemente 21,' one of
the greatest to ever play…

the wide world growing
three sizes smaller
that day.

Burn While Ye May

~ for Shannon Webster

"If your life is burning well,
poetry is just the ash."

We could count on Leonard Cohen
to have thought about it, before
committing that, or any other,
thought he thought to paper.

But, what about that ash…
what's left of a burning life.

As for me, I have 10,000
poems born of fire…
ashes duly returned
to the earth's skin.

The rare phoenix,
the one that rises
from the remains,
that's what books
are made from…

and no one'll ever
agree on the result.

And yet, as the earth
itself becomes a poem,
burning hotter and hotter,

the age will come when all
that is left behind will be…

the poems that stayed ashes.

Becoming John Denver

~ for Beth Melles and Audell Shelburne

"He was born in the summer
of his 27th year…" a strange
year to be born, I thought,
at the age of 7, or maybe 8,
but that *Rocky Mountain High*
LP was more than the sum of
vinyl and the diamond-toothed
needle in that console turntable.
I snapped. And, since becoming
Tarzan wasn't working out for me,
for logistic and geographic reasons,
all of a sudden I was "Coming home
to a place I'd never been before…"
and now, learning to play my older
brother's hand-me-down Silvertone
guitar consumed my little imagination.
John would want me in the band ASAP,
and my family would tell friends "He left
yesterday behind him, you might say he
was born again…" maybe through tears.
And though that didn't work out either,
you can see what came of it… this life
of mine unlocked, set free. You might
even say I found a key for every door.

A BLESSING FOR A BLESSING

~ for Rowan Forest Myers

Precious new soul,
breathing among us now,
the great mystery has given you
this family to be your holy allies in life,

living ancestors in spirit, who'll remind you
of the ancient ones and guide you toward
the sweet shadows of their generosity,
compassion, humility, and wisdom.

You were born of the stars,
a blessing for healing—
a fresh member of
the sacred trust,

handed down
through ages,
as steadfast
as a buffalo

under the moon
on the long horizon
of everything that you
are destined to become.

ANCHOR

~ for Anne Roberts

We don't see it
when it's doing
its best work...

somewhere down
at the deep-dark end
of a long and salty rope.

But knowing that it's there
helps us sleep in the rocking
of waves and hidden currents

that would, otherwise, carry us
off and far away from the plans
we had well-laid for the next day.

The Unspeakable

~ for Danna Primm

When the unspeakable
comes along, poetry
holds us in the wake
while we silently hunt
for what will eventually
need to be said… words
that will still be too much
to take when we say them.
But for now, let us *Be still…*
Listen to the stones of the wall…
so whispers the poem of one
rebellious old Trappist monk.
And let the quiet lick of flames
warm us for the coming night…
winter's balm for our shivering
hearts, says this wayward son.
So, dear sisters and brothers
of rock and fire, know that
some of the others gathered
here with us now are gut-deep
in need of your good thoughts,
even prayers if you have them…
but, remember not to speak them
out loud, until that time has come.

What It Is, and Isn't

~ for Lou Kohlman

Joy, like her sister,
Beauty, is forged of
time and the slow-burn
fire tended at the center of
a soul and the sacrifices it makes.

Happiness, like her best friend,
Fashion, lives on our surfaces,
fleeting... a smile made out
of ice and sex appeal, for
minds of lesser matter.

Happiness is too often
bought and collected, like
cars, stamps, jewelry, coins.

Joy comes with a price we never
expected to have to pay... and one
we were quite sure we couldn't afford,
but, now... one we'd gladly pay again.

Joy is a hidden garden, overgrown with
luscious ivy, a sanctuary for birds, a hut
for a silent old satisfied sage who picks
weeds with a glass of wine in his hand.

Happiness is a soccer stadium,
a Vegas casino, Fifth Avenue,
strolling the Champs-Élysées.

Joy is Saint Paul's Cathedral
standing among the smoke
and rubble up on Ludgate
Hill, in London's razed
center after the 1940
German Blitzkrieg.

A miraculous and
glorious survivor.

And What if It Is?

~ for Lou Kohlman

What if joy
is a decision...
instead of some
thing waited for?

What if joy exists,
like love, all around.
And the difference lies
in whether or not we choose
to focus our eyes on its miraculous
residue that turns out to be everywhere?

Like the blueberry juice that's staining
this very page, and my fingers. Yes...
even the unlikely wonder that some
tongue in south Texas could have
a chance to taste that blueberry.

It took me over fifty years to learn
that even stones manifest joy. Yes...
I have felt it with my own two hands.

And stones don't doubt its existence.
Only our species is capable of that.

What if rediscovering joy
has as much to do with
what it is we choose
to turn away from?

What if many billions
of dollars are spent each
quarter in the all-out effort
to keep us from ever finding joy
on our own, the joy here at our feet?
Because, if we did that, we would stop
scrambling every day to try and buy it?

So, the ultimate question might be:

    what if joy (like the ocean...
like dirt... and the mountains
    and trees) was here eons
before us, and is, therefore,
    as available to us as air?

Fermented Honey

~ for Anne Roberts, and the Fire Pit Sessions

For three years we've been straddling
the ferocious realignment of the way
we humans do our hygienic business
and daily modes of civic interaction.

We returned to caves, and fire pits,
and the fermented honey of poetry
and mead dripping into the flames.

We found ourselves by a live stream
we had no choice but to drink from.
And here at the shore of that stream
we lay anchor to share our stories…

to count something, anything besides
the number of dear souls we've lost.

And if I happened to be an anchor
for you? you have been ten times
that for me,
           tending the flame
that kept me warm, and alive.

WELL-SPRING

~ for Pegg Stoops, from Larry Smith

Well into her 80s,
what kept her young
was that never-ending
search for the next good
word from the current new
book she was forever reading.

One of those eager and ageless
souls… who hardly ever missed
those Third Thursday Readings…
always bringing the poetry of others
to impart before her own… a legacy
the rest of us should learn from, no?

She was a mighty oak of Oklahoma,
roots sunk deep into the dark-rich
soil of lines and stanzas, pages
and their paragraphs, leaves
that trace their shade-bearing
beauty back to the well-spring
of all of the earth's great stories.

Such a Thing

~ for Anne Roberts

Here, with a new year impending,
committing to kindness would be
more a revolution than it would
a resolution. Such a thing upon
which capitalism is not built—

considering what would be best
for someone else, one who is not
a stockholder—would stand out like
a child singing *Ave Maria* on a smoky
stage in some windowless strip club.

And yet… how would it ripple
the world if each of us gathered
around the fire here tonight were
to commit to this good suggestion
offered by one of our fellow flaming
souls who is determined to try and treat
the rest of us and others with more of it?

Kindness.

Can you imagine
the audacity…
the daring?

Spindrifting

~ for Larry Martin

Eventually,
there'll come
that steep, stony,
or sandy… or maybe
even wooden point where
the way becomes too watery,
and the only chance to continue
the journey is to grow wings,
or to sprout some fins.

WHY POETRY?

> ~ one for me,
> a gift from Miriam Rieck

Because, when you're alone together
way out in the woods you're always
wandering into (seems like decades
ago now), and Beauty finally takes
all of her clothes off, for a dare,
you've got to Do something
about it, my man... or die.

Because it was too late
to quit 20 years ago.

Because my mom
tells me I was born
with the mark of Cain.

Because it was the only way
that I could find to follow
in my father's footsteps.

Because of that time when
I played piano without the lights
on in a practice room at Norman High
School... and she silently slipped in
and sat beside me on the bench.

Because I believe in spirits
and angels, maybe even gods
and demons… and that they are
always doing things we can't control.

Because of that philosophy professor who
gave the final exam with only one question:
"Why?" And the only answers that got an
"A" were: "Because." and "Why not?"

Because, I still haven't found
the words I'm looking for.

Because I never could
have been a model
average-citizen.

And because,
mindlessness
simply must
be opposed.

POETRY: AN INDEX

> ~ for Shannon Webster

For Yehuda Amichai, it was a quarrel with God.

For Charles Bukowski, it was sifting through the madness for the Word, the sun inside him burning his gut.

For C. P. Cavafy, it was the great Yes within. But for Leonard Cohen, it was a Hallelujah he never finished.

For Stephen Dunn, it was to wander in the despoiled and radiant now, a better way to be alone, a troubled guest in his own house.

For Martín Espada, it began at twelve years old, refusing to recite the Pledge of Allegiance. Then, years later, it was remembering the *other* Alamo.

For Lawrence Ferlinghetti, it was the street-talk of angels and devils, the perfume of resistance.

For Allen Ginsberg, it was the best of minds, it was the worst of minds. But for Kahlil Gibran, it was a song that rises from a bleeding wound.

For Tony Hoagland, it was deciding what you're willing to kill, walking through the sunshine singing in chains. It was a mixture of good advice combined with slow-acting poison.

For Kobayashi Issa, it was a bubble in a cup of tea. It was the love-life of a cat.

For Robinson Jeffers, it was a thirty-year-old decision, the extraordinary patience of things, being always wakeful, steering through hell, his beloved coast of Carmel crying out for tragedy like all beautiful places, a willingness to burn his right hand in a slow fire to change the future.

For Jane Kenyon, it meant having it out with melancholy. It was sad flowers, the soul's bliss and suffering bound together, Galileo muttering under his beard.

For Federico García Lorca, it came from the first sob and the first kiss, the guitar

weeping, the cante jondo—a deep song,
and from a strange but simple folk who
sing hallucinated by a brilliant point of light
trembling on the horizon.

For Tony Mares, it was the fourth wound,
the wound of silence, a *tsin tsun*—his
hummingbird daughter flying off into the
agitated air of eternity, the guitar burning—
a silence where there was once music.

For Pablo Neruda, poetry arrived in search
of him. It was pure nonsense, the pure
wisdom of someone who knows nothing,
drunk with the great starry void.

For Sharon Olds, the poem was a vale of
soul-making, but also, her going back to
May 1937 and telling her parents to Stop,
don't do it—don't have children, and also,
she and her husband renewing their
promise to kill each other, but then, peace,
near the end of the world.

For Carl Phillips, it was the nothing
everything returns to, the knife, but also
what the knife has opened, the song we go
down singing.

For Leroy Quintana, it was the ocean
between him and his mother, but especially
that one moment in the jungle in Vietnam.
It was like true love and gasoline, missed
only when they run out.

For Rumi, it was finally knowing the
freedom of madness. It was that field, the
one out beyond ideas of wrongdoing and
rightdoing. It was donkey farts and
dancing… dancing, when you're broken
open… dancing, in your blood.

For William Stafford, it was thinking about
the knife, but then choosing otherwise.
It was a flower in the parking lot of the
Pentagon, junkyard crucifixes, and not
needing many words if you already know
what you're talking about. But certainly,
it was a ritual to read to each other.

For Lao Tzu, it was knowing what's
enough, when to stop. "Have done with
learning, And you will have no more
vexation." "He who knows does not speak.
He who speaks does not know." It was
teaching without talking, the empty space
within the vessel—what made it useful.

For Dylan Thomas, it was stumbling into that good night on the corner of Hudson and 11th, after the 18th shot of whiskey at the White Horse Tavern, his father, alas, having died despite his pleadings.

For Louis Untermeyer, it was a restless something half-seen, half-felt, the quiet church that smells of death. It was all beauty, perilous and grave.

For Paul Valéry, it was the spiny castellations and nacreous spirals of sea shells, the treasure of our ignorance at the feet of such natural wonders that we too often ruin with education. It was the pure sound rising above noise.

For Walt Whitman, it was, of course, the body electric, and that barbaric yawp, but also the end of priests, hovering in howls restrain'd by decorum. It was the bleeding drops of red, Where on the deck his Captain lies. But most certainly, it was that song of his self, that he sang over… and over…

For Xenokleides, it was exile in the 4th century BC—that and the ultimate poetic genius of having none of his works survive.

For W. B. Yeats, it was Maud Gonne, the Muse of his life, telling him that he was happy in his unhappiness—that's where all his beautiful poetry came from, so marrying her would do nothing but turn him into Samson with a shaved head.

For Adam Zagajewski, it was olive trees contorted in wild prayer. It was joy, the laughing sister of death. And it was as distant from us as we are from ourselves: a suffering older than Cain's. It held the thunder's echo. It was church towers resting on the ocean's floor. It was joy hiding despair, but under the despair— more joy. It was an altar before which no one prays, a duel that no one wins, a conversation without a final word…

The Last Poem

~ for Miriam Rieck

... will take us by surprise,
   and make us sad
   to see it go

... will not be any
   more widely read than
   the one that came before it

... will hold the answer... surely

... will be written with that last
   hot biscuit and cup of coffee

... will tell them what happened,
   but tell it slant... leaving a lot
   for alien imaginations to figure

... will at least be read by cockroaches

... will be on the bottom shelf of the
   very last rack in the very back
   row of the very last library

... will have the last word,

and the last laugh

... will be our epitaph

... will be my final rest...
and my eventual peace

... should be read out loud to
anyone, or no one, present

... will burn in fire... but not
the last fire... for there
will never be an end
to fire on earth

... will matter
as much as
the first one

... will be the wind
caressing the waves
of the one wild ocean
that finally rose too high
for us to continue treading
in remembrance of the divine
we were originally created to be.

Seriously, the Last Poem

~ for Miriam Rieck

I will write a thousand
of these, since death sits
around every corner, waits
just down every dark road,

you cannot be too careful.
And even in that inevitable
event, I won't be done yet.
I've requested my epitaph

to be, simply, an ellipsis…
those three little dots of all
that I left out… everything
I did not say forever ringing

in all the ready ears of those
whistling past me in the dark,
innocent wanderers whispering
"My God… he won't shut up."

Also by Nathan Brown

In the Days of Our Seclusion: March – May 2020
In the Days of Our Unrest: June – August 2020
In the Days of Our Undoing: September –
 November 2020
In the Days of Our Resilience: December 2020 –
 May 2021
Just Another Honeymoon in France:
 A Vagabond at Large
100 Years
An Honest Day's Prayer
An Honest Day's Ode
An Honest Day's Confession
I Shouldn't Say…
Arse Poetica
Apocalypse Soon
Don't Try (with Jon Dee Graham)
My Salvaged Heart: Story of a Cautious Courtship
To Sing Hallucinated:
 First Thoughts on Last Words
Oklahoma Poems, and Their Poets
Less Is More, More or Less
Karma Crisis: New and Selected Poems
Letters to the One-Armed Poet
My Sideways Heart
Two Tables Over
Not Exactly Job
Ashes over the Southwest
Suffer the Little Voices
Hobson's Choice

Author Bio

Nathan Brown is an author, songwriter, and award-winning poet living outside Wimberley, Texas. He holds a PhD in English and Journalism from the University of Oklahoma and taught there for over twenty years. He also served as Poet Laureate for the State of Oklahoma in 2013 and 2014.

He has published 26 books. Among them is *100 Years, To Sing Hallucinated: First Thoughts on Last Words*, and *Just Another Honeymoon in France: A Vagabond at Large*, a travel memoir that marks the first in a coming series.

His anthology *Oklahoma Poems, and Their Poets* was a finalist for the Oklahoma Book Award. *Karma Crisis: New and Selected Poems* was a finalist for the Paterson Poetry Prize. And his earlier book, *Two Tables Over*, won the 2009 Oklahoma Book Award.

For more, go to: **brownlines.com**

MEZCALITA PRESS

An independent publishing company
dedicated to bringing the printed poetry,
fiction, and non-fiction of musicians who
want to add to the power and reach
of their important voices.

For more, go to: **mezpress.com**

www.ingramcontent.com/pod-product-compliance
Lightning Source LLC
Chambersburg PA
CBHW020927090426
42736CB00010B/1066